TALES OF SOUTH AMERICAN FOOTBALL
PASSION, REVOLUTION AND GLORY

Tales of South American Football
Passion, Revolution and Glory

Jorge Knijnik

FAIRPLAY
PUBLISHING

Dedication

To my dearly missed parents Carlos and Olga,
who introduced me to the wonders
of South American culture—seeing and hearing
artist Mercedes Sosa singing her
passionate, revolutionary and glorious songs
through the streets and highways
of South America was undoubtedly the best
lesson anyone could wish for to learn
about our beloved and oppressed continent.

First published in 2024 by Fair Play Publishing
PO Box 4101, Balgowlah Heights, NSW 2093, Australia

www.fairplaypublishing.com.au

ISBN: 978-1-925914-35-1
ISBN: 978-1-925914-87-0 (ePub)

© Jorge Knijnik 2024
The moral rights of the author have been asserted.

All rights reserved. Except as permitted under the *Australian Copyright Act 1968* (for example, a fair dealing for the purposes of study, research, criticism or review), no part of this book may be reproduced, stored in a retrieval system, communicated or transmitted in any form or by any means without prior written permission from the Publisher.

Design and typesetting by Leslie Priestley.

Front cover illustration by Anastasiia Osypova.

All inquiries should be made to the Publisher via hello@fairplaypublishing.com.au

A catalogue record of this book is available from the National Library of Australia.

Contents

Foreword by Dr Andy Harper — 1
Introduction — 4

PART 1: PASSION — 9

Boca vs River: The world's most spicy clásico — 10
El Clásico Cafetero: The curious story of a tripartite coffee derby — 15
Tricampeões! The communist coach, the despot and the Seleção's third World Cup title — 20
The Most Painful Defeat: The 1982 Sarrià Tragedy and the demise of the *jogo bonito* — 27
Higuita, El Loco: A Colombian hero and a game-changer — 34
Azul y Oro, Maradona y Riquelme: Power, neoliberalism, and passion in *La Bombonera* — 41

PART 2: REVOLUTION — 53

The *Karimachus*: Bolivian women and the feminist battle in South American Football — 54
Smashing the Rules: Afonsinho and the end of players' slavery — 58
A Black Panther on the Field? Reinaldo, the goal-scorer who challenged a dictatorship — 64
Sócrates: Elegance and political fight—on and off the pitches — 70
No Mercy for Despots: The *hinchadas* with memory — 81
The Yellow Shirt Controversy: Social class struggle and the future of South American civilisation — 87

PART 3: GLORY 97

Glorious Marvels of South America 98
References 109
Acknowledgments 112
About the Author 113

Foreword

"It takes one to know one" is an English language proverb that is most commonly said with contempt. But in the case of this excellent book, wonderfully constructed by Professor Jorge Knijnik, it speaks to a more celebratory truth.

To the non-Latin world, South America is an exotic, intoxicating, magnetic mystery. A place shaped, in human terms, by centuries of competing cultures, forged by the impulses and legacies of European colonisation and waves of immigration, stricken by rapacious corruption, immobilised by financial dysfunction, energised by social eruption and revolution, soiled by despotic put-down .... and that's just Argentina! These themes wander, in various guises and at various times, through each part of the continent. And yet, despite the litany of negative headline-grabbing challenges, the spirit and generosity and beauty of the people continues to emanate, infecting visitors and wafting around the globe on the back of the various forms of dance, music and food.

Football, futbol, futebol. How to explain this *potpourri,* or at least get a sense of both the mayhem and the grandeur? In South America, this is both the question and the answer. How a game, imported by the English, could have so rapidly consumed the consciousness of an entire non-Anglo population—such that it defines the daily fluctuations of the entire place—is truly a phenomenon. Sure, there are other (most) places in the world that have a deep and abiding connection to this (most) beautiful game. But apart from the mechanical and organisational genius of the European versions of football, the real wonder and majesty and art has historically been the preserve of South America. The world's great(est) players and, at any given point, the world's most powerful teams (the ubiquity of Brazil in this category shouldn't need to be pointed out) hail from this vast and diverse place.

But the on-field wonder that has transfixed the fans of the game and sent its businesspeople into a frenzy is only part of the story. Football in South America is life—it is death—and it is every single thing in between.

To understand South America, or even come close to such an epiphany, one must understand its football, and "it takes one to know one". Few are as well placed as Jorge Knijnik, a football fan/academic of impressive note, who was born in and crafted by Brazil's version of South America. It takes someone who is fluent in the mother tongue, in this case South America and football, to be able to explain this confluence to those outside who seek to look in.

I am one such person. I love lots of places around the world. I really love South America. Australian football icon, the late Johnny Warren, 'chaperoned' a few of us to one of his favourite haunts, Rio de Janeiro, on a World Cup-qualifying trip that saw the Australian national team lose a final inter-confederation play-off to the Alvaro Recoba-inspired Uruguay in 2001. So, before Johnny could get us to Rio, we of course spent our first week in Montevideo, preparing for and then watching the last-ditch match. Montevideo was incredible. And it served as a life-enhancing prelude to the Rio sojourn whose impact was utterly profound on me. It was just over two weeks that permeated my consciousness, irrevocably. Upon departure, I found myself stocking up on musical CDs (remember them?) of tango and pagode (a Rio musical style that's a sub-genre of samba). For God's sake, what was this?! I still remember, like it was yesterday, the gloom and frustration at the Estadio Centenario on the fateful football day when Recoba and his men sliced through the hopes of the Australian team and booked their place at the 2002 World Cup Finals. My hurt wasn't so much that we lost. That was bad enough. But for this Australian football lover and television broadcaster, it was something more. It was the realisation that we, us, Australia, had no right to take this football away from Uruguay. That the fortunes for La Celeste, or of Nacional or Danubio or Peñarol meant everything.

For an Australian who sings along with our national anthem, invoking images of being in a land "girt by sea", La Celeste line up to the spine-tingling *"Orientales, la patria o la tumba" ("People, the fatherland or the grave")*. Girt by sea vs laying down your life—which is more evocative? As crestfallen as I was, a broken shell of a patriot, it was also the birth of a new insight. Then, as fortune would have it, Australia would play Uruguay again, at the same final stage of qualifying, four years later for the 2006 Finals. At the Australian second-leg of the two-game series, Recoba was quoted as saying that a Finals' berth was Uruguay's *right*. The Australian press was up in arms. The radio shock jocks were having a field day. "What is Uruguay? Hell, they don't even speak English, how dare Recoba declare such ridiculous pomposity!" And as the media's teeth gnashed away and Australia nearly drowned in its navel-gazing and cultural insecurity, I think I knew what he meant, (sort of). I saw it in the kids at Centenario four years earlier. For Uruguay, for Recoba, the game is *everything* and he sensed, very perceptively I'd say, that in his view Australia would rise and move on without football. Uruguay wouldn't. Not completely. Not totally. Not without scarring and serious disfigurement.

This is certainly not to say that any singular experience can provide the necessary immersion to comprehend the magnitude and complexity of culture. Far from it. But it can be the catalyst to want to understand more. To dig deeper. To open up. To listen, watch, read and play. This book is one such vehicle.

I met Jorge in the process of completing my doctoral research which, coincidentally, centred on Australian football and culture. His ability to synthesize the topic, from a non-Australian background, was impressive. I very much appreciated the feedback and support he offered which of course was fortified by his own impressive academic investigations and writing.

Jorge takes us into the world of his heritage. By reading this book, you will leave with a greater sense of peace and appreciation and be just that little bit closer to the essence of the mystery that is South America and its football.

Passion, revolution and glory, indeed. Muito obrigado, Jorge, abraços.

Andy Harper, PhD
Dr Andy Harper is a former national league player in Australia, longstanding professional TV commentator on men's and women's football, and youth coach. He is the author of four books on football including two co-authored with the late Johnny Warren MBE and Ange Postecoglou.

Introduction

"Years have gone by and I've finally learned to accept myself for who I am: a beggar for good football. I go about the world, hand outstretched, and in the stadiums I plead: 'A pretty move, for the love of God.' And when good football happens, I give thanks for the miracle and I don't give a damn which team or country performs it."
—**Eduardo Galeano**

It is common to say that football in South America is "more than a game" as it is woven through the social and political fabric of all South American societies. Nevertheless, we do not need to travel far, nor go back many years, to see that politics and football are entangled not only in South America, but across all continents, and at every single step of the game. We only have to look at the latest two FIFA Men's World Cups (2018 and 2022) to see all of the political and economic decisions that permeated the choices of Russia and Qatar as hosts of football's mega event.

Nonetheless, in South America the political aspects of the game are more extensive than anywhere else. Initially, we must acknowledge that football politics impact the average South American citizen's life with a strength rarely seen in other places. Former players use their popularity acquired on the field to become elected members in their Parliaments. While this phenomenon also happens in other places—for example, when Chelsea idol and 1995 Ballon D'or George Weah became the elected President of Liberia in 2017, or when the 1974 World Cup Golden Boot winner Grzegorz Lato was elected as a Senator in Poland—the politics–football nexus goes further in South America. For example, it's possible that a popular club's president who has never played the game can use their position to develop their political career and gain great power, as in the case of the former Boca Junior and then Argentinian President (2015–2019), Mauricio Macri.

Moreover, though, if football around the world is used as a political tool to elect government and Parliamentary officers, in South America it has been weaponized as an ultimate tool to, on the one hand, promote authoritarian government; and, on the other, to critique, question and even overthrow tyrannies that have sprung up across the subcontinent for several decades. South Americans have taken the political extent of this game to another level, and, by using their popular rhythms and dances, subverted what once was the 'colonizers' game' in a way that has been marvelling the world for decades. Football is part of the everyday life of South American peoples: our language, our costumes, food, popular songs—all aspects of our practical and symbolic life have a connection to the game.

This is what the tales in this book aim to recount. Each chapter tells a story of how football intertwines with political fights, social class struggles and cultural elements within different countries in the region. From national team shirts used to support extremist politicians, to coffee production; from social protests to the feminist revolution; wherever you turn your gaze in South America, there is a football backstory waiting to be told.

However, these stories cannot be told as if they are ordinary events. For the last few decades, football tales have been and continue to be experienced in a unique South American style. They are passionate accounts, embedded in revolutionary action and glorious happenings in the social history of the subcontinent. Hence, this book brings sparks of the true meaning of the game for different South American communities.

It is structured around three main themes: *passion, revolution, and glory*.

Part 1: *Pasión* (Spanish for passion)—contains six stories that illustrate South Americans' extreme passion and entrenched love for football. Initially, there are two stories about local derbies. The first highlights a fiery Argentinian *clásico* that is well-known around the world. I show that both *Xeneizes* and *Millonarios* (Boca Juniors and River Plate supporters, respectively) have an inseparable and intense connection to their local derby that goes far beyond the stadiums. The second story reveals the unusual story of a derby with three teams, and how it links to the everyday cultural and working life of significant Colombian communities.

Next, there are two stories about two Brazilian national teams that are still admired and cheered around the football planet: the 1970 Seleção, with João Saldanha, its 'nearly' coach who challenged the dictatorship and planted the seeds for a team that revolutionized the strategies of contemporary football. Their impacts are still being felt on the pitch today. Following the chronicle of that victorious side is the story of the 1982 Brazilian team which, regardless of its on-field results, are still seen by many nostalgic football lovers as the last true representatives of the *jogo bonito*.

Next, you will learn how a Colombian goalkeeper changed not only the way we currently play the game, but also its rules, transforming present-day football to make it a more tense and faster game. Wrapping up Part 1 is a story of a passionate dispute which pitted two idols of one of the greatest South American clubs.

Part 2: *Revolución* (Spanish for revolution) contains six chapters where you will learn about the diverse elements of subversion that played a central role in the development of the game in South America. To open, there is no better choice than writing about the feminist revolution that is currently taking place across the South American footballing milieu. The story of the Bolivian *karimachus* clearly exemplifies the power of football as a social and political means to promote gender equity in the continent. Then, the following pages chronicle three distinctive players—Afonsinho, Reinaldo and Sócrates—who each challenged the tyrannical ruling of powerful and dangerous dictators on and off the fields. The next chapter highlights how football supporters and clubs' members and families were damaged during the dictatorships in Uruguay, Chile and Argentina, and how the sport is helping with the ongoing process of transitional justice that has been occurring in these countries since the end of their authoritarian governments. Part 2 closes with the details of how a national football jersey mobilized intense political passions in the largest South American country, and how it was usurped by a large political faction to have its powerful meaning diluted to become a symbol of conservatism and violence. The chapters in Part 2 are evidence of the deep entanglement of politics and football in South America.

Part 3: *Al final la Gloria* is the concluding section of the book. Its sole chapter narrates the footballing wonders that two South American football geniuses have generously offered to the world. It serves as an illustration of the meaning of the book: after many passionate revolutions, South Americans shall achieve football glory.

These tales are not the 'definitive guide of South American football history', nor do they provide its absolute sociological interpretation. Rather, the stories woven into this book aim to give the reader a taste of how football is lived in the joyful but oppressed communities across the countries of this exploited subcontinent.

Even though the book is divided into three different sections, at the end you might reach the same conclusion that South Americans have learned over decades of playing and breathing this magnificent game in their daily lives: that *pasión*, *revolución* and *gloria* coexist and it is their combination that contributes to the creation of one of the most beautiful shows on Earth: South American football.

Dr. Jorge Knijnik

PART 1:
PASSION

CHAPTER 1

Boca vs River: The world's most spicy clásico

In 2011, Ole Christian Madsen, an award-winning Danish film director, launched a romantic comedy called *Superclásico*. With its action taking place in the streets of Buenos Aires, the Argentinian capital city, the plot of the movie tells a story of Christian, a Danish wine retailer whose wife abandoned him and fled to Argentina to live with a football star who played for one of the most important South American clubs. Wretched by losing his wife, Christian then flies to Argentina to try to convince his wife to come back to him. He is not aware that he would land in the city during the week leading up to one of the biggest events in the country: the *Superclásico*.

Boca Juniors vs River Plate. This is one of the world's biggest sports rivalries. Around the globe, it is very hard to find a greater, lengthier (the first *Superclásico* was played in 1908*)* and more contentious football match than the Buenos Aires *Superclásico*, the *porteño* super derby. Both Argentinians clubs carry a centenary history; the two originated at the beginning of the 20th century in La Boca, a *villa*, a poor and humble slum in the south of the Argentinian capital city. In the 1920s, River Plate relocated to the north of the city, but the dispute of the true representatives of the lower classes, the workers from *La Boca* remained—even though nowadays both clubs have supporters across all social classes in the country.

The *Superclásico* stops the nation. Every local, regional or national newspaper, and every radio or TV station broadcasts the pre-match news—a week prior to the game. During match day, the *Barra Bravas*—the fanatic Argentinian *ultras* who stand for the whole match and never rest supporting their team—put a big show together in the stands with their fireworks, chants, flags, tifos and dance. Then, after the match, there are several more days of talking about the results, the supporters' behaviour and everything related to the derby. The country, and its capital city, breathes the *Superclásico* for a whole fortnight. Can you imagine what would happen if these teams were to compete against each other more than once a month?

2015: an unforgettable *Superclásico*

Due to their proximity, Boca and River can meet regularly with multiple matches scheduled without much space between them; things tend to get spicy with the rival clubs and their fans. This was exactly what happened in 2015. Boca Juniors and River Plate faced each other in early May in a top-of-the table clash in the Argentinian Primera División (first tier) - Boca won 2-0; after that, in a space of just few weeks, they played again, twice, in a knock-out phase of the *Copa Libertadores de America* (the South American Champions League). The *Superclásico* dominated the news and the country's street and pub talk for over three weeks. After the knock-out matches, one club would stay alive in the competition, while the other would 'die'.

Unfortunately, this metaphor nearly became true. Violent scenes of the second *Libertadores* match were revealed to the world at the *Bombonera* (Boca Juniors' home stadium). The score was even (0–0) at half-time. River had won the first leg by 1-0 and were playing better than their opponents in the second. After the interval, as the River Plate players were walking through the tunnel that connects the change rooms to the fields, several tear gas bombs were thrown inside. Four River Plate players were severely burned, and others were also affected. After a heated on-field argument between officials from both sides, and then nearly 60 minutes of deliberations, the match was finally suspended.

Rapidly, the mainstream media propagated that Boca Juniors' *Barra Bravas* had thrown the gas bombs. The press even suggested that one subgroup of the Boca Juniors' supporters, from a city called *Lomas de Zamora*, could have committed the crime—as they were upset due to the small number of tickets that they were given to watch the match by Boca's president. Prior to the super derby, they were sending notices and threats to both clubs, saying that something could happen on the

Superclásico match day. However, nothing was proven against this group. On the contrary, with the aid of TV cameras, the police investigations discovered that the main culprit of this violent act was a Boca supporter (a *Xeneize*) who was well-known within the club. Nicknamed as *El Panadero* (the Baker) as his father owned several bakeries in Buenos Aires, Adrian Napolitano was a Boca Juniors member. He was also affiliated with a political group within Boca Juniors whose leader was a bitter enemy of Boca's former president—then Buenos Aires Mayor and later Argentina's President: Mauricio Macri.

The CONMEBOL (South American Football Federation) took harsh measures against Boca Juniors due to *El Panadero's* ferocious acts: the club was eliminated from that year's Libertadores de America; received a US$200K fine and was forced to play four of its home matches under closed doors, plus another four matches as visitors with no supporters. *El Panadero* was quick to declare his regret over his acts, saying he had been a fan for over 20 years, and was a family man and a hard worker who had acted without thinking. But the fact remained that his political group was in opposition to Boca's board at that time. Argentinian newspapers speculated for weeks about the 'real political motivation' of that attack.

The 2015 turmoil in the *Superclásico* is relevant for this derby's history because regardless of *El Panadero's* real motivations, it clearly demonstrates how football and politics are entwined in the *Superclásico's* ethos. 2015 was a Presidential election year in Argentina. A few months after the Libertadores match, Argentinians were to go to the polls. The Mayor of Buenos Aires (the nation's capital city) was Mauricio Macri, who had earlier served as Boca Juniors president between 1995 and 2007. Macri was the main candidate for the Argentinian right wing in the 2015 Federal elections. Furthermore, Daniel Angelici, then president of Boca Juniors, was an ally of Macri and supported his Presidential ambitions.

Coincidentally, Angelici was not seen on the field while that May 2015 *Superclásico* was paralysed due to the tear gas. He even 'disappeared' from the news. Mainstream media channels—such as *Clarín* and *La Nación*—that at that time had a clearly anti-government agenda, avoided naming or criticising Boca's president over the super derby's incident. They also never mentioned his relationships with the *Barra Bravas'* subgroups. In addition, Angelici made no comments on *Fox Sports*, hence being somewhat protected in the moment of crisis.

Macri, Angelici and their media allies always knew that loyal *Barra Bravas* fans—and the criminals who have infiltrated them—represent numerous powerful groups in Argentina. Politicians from all parties want to have them on their side. Football fans have an important say not only in the country's sporting life, but also in its political affairs. Boca Juniors and River Plate have more than 30 million supporters combined, which represents nearly 70% of all football fans in the country.

The real election

Two months after the Presidential election, Boca Juniors elected its new president. Across the slums of *La Boca*, the rumours were that this was the most important election, the only one that really mattered. With the support of newly elected Argentinian President Mauricio Macri, Daniel Angelici was re-elected to the club's presidency with 44% of the votes. He continued at the top of Boca Juniors until 2019.

Undoubtedly, both elections had a strong connection. Buenos Aires, once known as a European city in South America due to its high social and cultural standards, now has a great deal of poverty, social decline and urban violence; on the other hand, as a Mayor and then as a President, Mauricio Macri promoted an excellent atmosphere for the business of major construction companies and real estate, as well as for the development of international corporations within the country's economy.

Since Macri's term as Boca Junior's presidential chair (1995–2007) Boca Juniors' presidents have used the violent behaviour of the *Barra Bravas* as an excuse to try and proceed with their plans of taking down the historical, mythical and popular *La Bombonera* Stadium. Situated in the heart of *La Boca*, they wanted to pull down one of the world's most iconic football stadiums to erect a new and modern arena for the club. They wanted to promote an even bigger commodification of Argentinian football that was very much aligned to their corporate allies' plans and ambitions: new stadiums always generate very good business!

However, their projects faced ongoing resistance across the La *Boca* neighbourhood—*'de Bombonera no nos vamos!'*—'we won't leave the *Bombonera*

Stadium!' was the motto of loyal fans, painted as graffiti on the walls of *La Boca*. The fans could not send a clearer message to the neoliberal club's management, who were agents of 'modern football'.

With a football background to its plot, the Danish film that had the Boca vs River match as its title portrays Argentine culture in an unusual and fun way, and it has an emotional and romantic ending. The Superclásico movie was as successful as the actual Buenos Aires derby: in 2012, Madsen's movie was nominated as one of the nine entries for that year's Oscars for Best Foreign Language Film.

However, what the movie could not portray was whether Argentinians would be able to push for a less aggressive atmosphere within football, or if they would be able to keep their traditions and their football passion in such a tainted environment. It would take longer than anyone's wishes for Argentinians to be reunited, without violence, within their stadiums. At the same time, they are still looking to deal with real criminal behaviour in football—which is clearly not only perpetrated by Barra Bravas from the streets, but also by high level suits in their air-conditioned offices.

CHAPTER 2

El Clásico Cafetero: The curious story of a tripartite coffee derby

Coffee drinkers both in the Global North and the Global South have been relishing the astonishing flavours and scents of café colombiano (Colombian coffee) for decades. Known by many specialists as the world's best coffee, the café colombiano is one of the largest export products from Colombia where a range of premium varieties is cultivated and distributed throughout the world. Nearly 100% of the coffee produced in Colombia comes from Arabica beans that are known for giving the light, sweet, and extravagant savour that countless coffee fans hanker for.

The most suitable regions to grow the best Arabica beans are the ones that have a temperate climate. Arabica seeds dislike large day-time temperature variations. They also favour regions with well-determined rainy and dry periods, and particularly thrive in higher altitudes. These are some of the reasons why the coffee industry has grown so strongly in the Colombian Andean region (La Cordillera de Los Andes). This is where the Eje Cafetero[1] (the Coffee Axis) is located.

Colombia is geopolitically organized in 32 departments (the equivalent of 'states'), and one capital district (Bogotá D.C.). Situated in the west of the country in the Andean region, the Eje Cafetero is located in between the three most important capital cities in Colombia: Bogota, Medellin and Cali.

The Eje Cafetero includes the departments of Caldas, Risaralda and Quindío that were formed by the 1966 division of the old department called Viejo Caldas. A car trip from the capital city of Bogotá to the Eje Cafetero takes around seven hours.

------

[1] *Cafetero* is a Spanish word that can be translated as something related to coffee. In addition, it can mean someone who is a heavy coffee drinker; a coffee fan. Furthermore, it can designate a person whose job is to grow coffee and trade with it, or a coffee shop owner. It can be used to talk about the coffee market *(el mercado cafetero)* and in its feminine form *(cafetera)* it means a coffee-maker machine.

It is a wonderful and safe region of Colombia, with colourful and vibrant cities such as Filandia and amazing mountain landscapes that offer incredible hiking opportunities. Tourists can visit coffee farms in the region to learn all the steps involved in coffee production—from its inception to manual harvest and exportation. These coffee farms also enable you to understand the social impact of the coffee business for the region. Given its tradition, sustainable and productive features, in 2011 UNESCO declared the coffee cultural landscape of Colombia to be a place of intangible cultural heritage based on World Heritage Convention principles.

As in other regions and departments of Colombia, football has a special place in the hearts of Colombians who live in one of the three departments of the Eje Cafetero region. However, football in the region has a feature that is quite unique not only in the Colombian sporting landscape, but also within the global sports arena. It is the Clásico Cafetero (the Cafetero derby).

Derbies

During the 18th century, young men from neighbouring parishes used to be involved in highly unruly games to push a ball into the adjacent parish. This was the origin of football. The most famous of these games used to be played in the city of Derby in the county of Derbyshire, England. The competition used to run between the All Saints' parish and their neighbour, Saint Peters. Since then, derby rivalries have spread around the world and are especially known for their intense (and sometimes brutal) atmosphere. The orthodox definition of a 'derby' states that these are contests between two teams from the same city. These days though, two teams that are not from the same town but play in the same region and have the prospect to play each other on a regular basis can also claim that their matches are a 'derby'.

Every football follower knows that derbies are singular matches. Derbies have the unique power to explore human beings' 'us vs them' feelings and mentality like nothing else. Even when fans cannot follow their team during their other seasonal matches, they save money to attend the derby. Derbies literally divide cities in two different coloured halves. The well-known 'Old Firm' derby (or the Glasgow derby, where Rangers play Celtic) is deemed by many football traditionalists as the world's biggest derby. Nowadays, world famous derbies such as the Manchester derby (City vs United) or El Derbi Madrileño (the Madrid derby, where Real versus Atlético) fill countless hours and pages of sporting news and generate numerous debates for weeks both before and after the event. Derbies are also a major source of revenue for their clubs.

South American football features many world-known clásicos (derbies), such as the Superclásico between Boca Juniors and River Plate in Buenos Aires and the memorable FlaxFlu (Flamengo vs Fluminense) in Rio de Janeiro, or the match that features the most important Uruguayan sides in Montevideo: Peñarol y Nacional, which is also known as 'El Superclásico'. In Colombia, you can enjoy a range of clásicos across the country's different regions. For example, the famous El Clásico Paisa that happens in Medellín city between Atletico Nacional and Independiente Medellín; or the Bogotá derby in the capital city known as 'El Clásico Bogotano' that opposes the well-supported Millonarios and the Independiente Santa Fe. In most of the world's derbies, fans are excited to see their own team playing their fiercest rivals—many times winning a local derby means more for a fan than being a finalist at a national competition.

The Eje Cafetero also has its own derby. However, as if imitating the originality and uniqueness of their regional coffee, the Clásico Cafetero sees not only two teams in opposition, but three! It is unique in the international football scene. As the region known as 'the Coffee Axis' is made up of three departments—Caldas, Risaralda and Quindío, the matches between the main teams from the capital cities of these states are called El Clásico Cafetero—the Coffee Axis derby.

Of course, these three teams do not play each other at the same time (even by any creative Colombian standards, this would mean going far beyond the limits!). The three clubs that may be involved in a Clásico Cafetero are Once Caldas (the team from Manizales, the capital city of the department of Caldas), the Deportivo Pereira (from Pereira, Risaraldas's capital city) and lastly the Deportes Quindío (from Armenia, the capital city of the Quindío department).

The conflicts between the three capital cities of the Eje Cafetero are grander than mere football rivalries; they are economic and political and go back to the time when they all belonged to the department of Viejo Caldas in the 20th century.

Then, the cities of Armenia and Pereira used to complain that the capital Manizales did not send them enough resources to fund their necessities, such as new schools and health centres. Nowadays, these rivalries are still alive, mostly in the cultural, social and sporting arenas.

Among the three teams, Once Caldas is the one that is the most successful, not only when playing its Cafetero rivals, but also in both national and international contexts. By the end of 2022, Once Caldas and Deportivo Pereira had faced each other 219 times; with the Manizales' side on 85 wins and the Pereira squad on 63; the two teams had drawn their matches on 71 occasions. Their first meeting was in 1949 when then-named Deportes Caldas defeated Deportivo Pereira 5–4. The rivalry between Deportes Quindío and Deportivo Pereira is more balanced, with nearly the same number of victories for each side (85 vs 87) and 55 draws. Their first match took place in 1951 when the team from Pereira won the Clásico 4–2.

Once Caldas has won the Colombian national league four times, from the first title in 1950, when it was still called Deportes Caldas. Once Caldas became internationally well-known in 2004 when they won the Copa Libertadores de America, eliminating major Brazilian clubs such as Santos and São Paulo during their campaign, and defeating South American powerhouse Boca Juniors in a two-legged Final, where after two drawn matches, Once Caldas won the title in a penalty shootout. In December of that year, the Colombian side travelled to Japan to play Porto FC in the Intercontinental Cup. After draws in both regular and extra time, Once Caldas were defeated 8–7 in a penalty shootout.

Even though it is yet to achieve national and international glory, Deportivo Pereira has left its mark on Colombian football. It was founded in 1944, and since 1949 it has been playing in the national competition (which started a year earlier), either in its first or second tier. Deportivo Pereira was three times placed third in the Colombian championship (1952, '62 and '66) and in 2021 was runner-up in the Colombian Cup. It has won the second-tier national competition three times.

Deportes Quindío was created in 1951 and in its initial years, it collected some national silverware. After finishing runner-up in the National Championship in 1953 and '54, it won the title in 1956. For most of its existence, Deportes Quindío has played in the first national tier (Primera A), but on nine occasions it has been relegated to the second tier (Primera B), most recently in 2021.

Regardless of each club's record of wins, defeats and titles, the uniqueness of a three-way derby is another wonder of South American (and Colombian) football. As they do with their marvelous coffee, perhaps the Eje Cafetero could spread and export this idea around the world, creating more exciting opportunities for football fans to celebrate their teams?

CHAPTER 3

Tricampeões! The communist coach, the despot and the Seleção's third World Cup title

Tricampeões! Three-time world champions! Seated on his dad's lap, a four-year-old boy joined the large car parade across São Paulo city that celebrated another world title for the Brazilian team—this time at the Estadio Azteca in Mexico City. The boy was totally free to press the car's horn as he wished, adding his small contribution to the already super-loud noise in the crowded streets. On his right side, his mum waved the Brazilian flag he had coloured while everybody watched Pelé & co.'s team defeat the team in blue—the *Azzurri*.

The year was 1970. It was the first time that a World Cup game was being broadcast live to the Brazilian population. Prior to that, football fans would gather collectively to listen to football matches around a large radio, either placed in a pub on a window facing the street or in the centre of their lounge room. Football aficionados would listen to the matches with their ears glued to a pocket radio. The images of thousands of fans listening to their portable devices as they watched a match in the Maracanã Stadium are part of Brazilian football folklore. It did not matter too much whether they were comfortably seated in a VIP area or standing behind the goals; middle-aged and elderly men were keen for the radio commentators to verbally unfold the football drama that was happening in front of their eyes.

Emílio Garrastazu Médici, then the country's military dictator, used the portable radio to build a 'people's man' image. Under his leadership that lasted almost five years (October 1969 to March 1974), the country endured the harshest period of its 21-year military dictatorship. Known as the *'Years of Lead'* during Médici's presidential term, nearly any political dissent in Brazil was silenced: armed guerrillas were physically exterminated with hundreds of government-endorsed assassinations; opponents were tortured and killed inside police headquarters, and many bodies are yet to be recovered and brought back to their families; furthermore, hundreds of Brazilians were forced into political exile abroad. However, as the press was under strict censorship, ordinary citizens had no clue about what was happening in their country. They only knew that they could not vote to elect their representatives at any level. In addition, most could only read or see censored newspapers whose headlines displayed the country's 'economic miracle', together with the army's wins against the 'communist terrorists' who were arguably plaguing the nation.

In the meantime, pictures of Médici listening to football matches on his portable radio were strategically spread on TV channels and on the front pages of the country's major newspapers. The dictatorship's propaganda team were clearly mixing football and politics. When the winning *Seleção* came back from Mexico, the whole team was welcomed in the country's capital (Brasilia), and players received government money directly to their recently created savings accounts. The images of Carlos Alberto Torres, the team's captain, wearing a nice suit and handing the world's *tricampeonato* (third championship) trophy to Médici became famous and were shown all over the country.

A few players, such as Pelé and Carlos Alberto, developed a close relationship with the dictator who started to send them birthday cards. Many years later after the country's re-democratization, Carlos Alberto alleged that this gesture did not mean he supported the regime. According to him, in the 1970s he was young, only interested in playing football, and knew nothing about politics.

Tostão, the player who might have invented the 'false-nine' role in football, seconded his captain's words, stating that the players focused intensely on the World Cup tournament—without any political concerns. Like the rest of the population, they only became aware of the army's atrocities much later. However, just a few weeks prior to boarding the flight to Mexico, Tostão had voiced his criticisms of the censorship imposed by the regime on the Brazilian media. After his opinion was published in the *Pasquim*, the only independent weekly newspaper in the country in that period, Tostão was firmly advised to keep silent if he wanted to play in the 1970 World Cup tournament.

João Saldanha: the coach who should have been the champion

Many say that Médici actually enjoyed the sport and understood football tactics. His alleged game knowledge was such that during the Seleção's preparation for the 1970 tournament, he tried to interfere with their roster, pushing then coach João Saldanha to select a few players in the team. Among them was Médici's so-called favourite striker, *Dadá Maravilha* (Dario the Marvel). Saldanha then went to the press and declared that "Médici did not ask my opinion to form his ministerial cabinet; I don't need his opinion to put my team together". Two weeks after this statement, João Havelange, the then president of the Brazilian Sports Confederation (CBD), fired Saldanha and his coaching assistants.

A few days after Saldanha's sacking, a football lottery was regulated in Brazil. Approved by the military government and controlled by the Federal Bank, the profits from this national and widespread football gambling went straight to the CBD's coffers. The lottery income swiftly became CBD's core financial resource. The Brazilian team's campaign for the World Cup—and maybe other operations too—was boosted with the lottery funding. More than a month prior to the tournament, the playing team travelled to *Guanajuato* to adjust to the heights of the adjacent *Guadalajara* city where the first phase of the World Cup was to be played. The political agreement that funded this long-term preparation allowed the team to greatly improve their fitness, as evidenced by 64% of their goals being scored in the second half in the 2,000 meters-high *Guadalajara* city.

Zagallo, who played for the Seleção in the 1958 and 1962 World Cup-winning campaigns and was then coaching *Botafogo de Futebol e Regatas*, a major Brazilian club from Rio de Janeiro, was appointed as the national team's head coach after Saldanha's sacking. He immediately included *Dadá Maravilha* in his roster, demonstrating a feature of his coaching career: being a yes-man, always bent on pleasing people in power. However, to be fair, *Dadá* never set foot on a Mexican field during the 1970 World Cup tournament.

Nevertheless, several military personnel joined both the coaching group and the national team's staff. Among them were Claudio Coutinho, a well-regarded army fitness Captain to lead the team's endurance program; the retired Brigadier Jerônimo Bastos, who already had a commanding position at the CBD as the Head of Delegation. Furthermore, Major Roberto Câmara Lima Ypiranga de Guaranys was appointed as the Chief of Security for the Seleção. Guaranys was then the 'President's man' within the staff, reporting directly to Médici about the team's day-to-day activities. After the country's re-democratization, Guaranys was denounced as a torturer by the Official Commission of Truth.

Many years later, Havelange opened up about Saldanha's firing, saying he could not resist Médici's pressure to fire the coach. The *Dadá Maravilha* affair could be deemed the last straw that broke up an already challenging and somewhat paradoxical relationship between Saldanha and the military dictatorship's high command. Many years later, Saldanha also declared that *Dadá* was just an excuse invented by the dictatorship as Médici had never actually seen 'the Marvel' playing. Saldanha was a member of the Communist Party, and a killing despot such as Médici would never tolerate a self-professed political opponent as Saldanha in a coaching role that could give him an even higher visibility if the team came back home with the Jules Rimet trophy from Mexico in 1970.

The timeline is clear. Top guerrilla chief and Communist Party leader, Carlos Marighella, was ambushed and murdered by the political police on the streets of São Paulo city in November 1969. In January 1970, still as the Seleção's coach, Saldanha went to the World Cup draw in Mexico City. Enraged by his friend's cowardly execution, Saldanha presented a dossier to the international audience, denouncing the ongoing torture and killing of political opponents in Brazil. This was the real last straw for him. In March, after an intense backdoor campaign led by Médici's staff, Saldanha was sacked.

Saldanha did not have a traditional coach trajectory. He was born in 1917 in the city of *Alegrete* in the southernmost Brazilian state of Rio Grande do Sul. Alegrete had a fierce football rivalry with *Bagé*, the neighbouring city where coincidentally Médici was born. It was rare that the two cities' football teams played without a big brawl either during or after the contest. As a child, Saldanha's family had to move to nearby Uruguay to escape political disturbances in the early years of the Brazilian Republic. Returning to Rio de Janeiro, he played for the Botafogo youth team before going to Law School. He did not finish the course, but it was at the University that he started to get closer to communist ideologies, becoming a member of the Brazilian Communist Party (PCB) and befriending some of its future leaders.

In the early 1950s, Saldanha became one of the most acclaimed sports journalists in the country. Deemed as having an unparalleled tactical view over the game, people started to ask whether he would be better placed as a real football coach. In 1957, despite never holding a similar role before, he started his coaching career as the head coach of Botafogo where great names such as Garrincha were playing. Winning the 1957 state title, he remained as Botafogo's coach for two years, before moving back to his career in sports journalism.

In the late 1950s and during the 1960s, Saldanha turned into the most influential sports voice of the country. The late 1960's football crisis engulfing the country helped him on his move back to the coaching bench. After winning two consecutive World Cup titles (1958 and 1962), the Brazilian supporters were keen to claim a hat-trick of World Cups. However, their failure in the 1966 World Cup, hosted and won by England, where the team did not get through the group phase, immersed Brazilian football in a huge and lasting economic and managerial disaster. In the early months of 1969, the CBD made a surprising but astute move: they invited Saldanha to be Seleção's head coach. This invitation was quite a shock given the sporting body's alignment with the right-wing authoritarian government—Saldanha's communist allegiances and opposition to the political regime were well-known. On the other hand, it was also a clever move, as it was a clear attempt to shut the critical voices in the media.

Saldanha had a short but triumphant term as the Seleção's head coach. His 'beasts', as he used to call his team's players—names such as Pelé, Tostão, Gerson, Rivelino and others – easily passed through the South American qualifiers, winning six out of their six matches, scoring 23 and conceding just two goals. The Brazilian supporters' heart was again full of pride for their rehabilitated national team.

Nevertheless, the military were closely monitoring the CBD and Saldanha's movements. They knew that the CBD had serious financial issues, and were aware that Saldanha, also known as 'John the Fearless', would never retreat from his political position. Their anger grew when they heard his denunciation of the dictatorship's crimes against humanity. When the *Dadá Maravilha* opportunity (or excuse?) presented itself, they threw all their power behind the suggestion and pushed for his sacking.

Saldanha knew he would not last in the position. In a 1985 TV interview, he admitted he considered Médici 'the number one killer in Brazil's history'. Furthermore, in the same interview, he declared that in the months that preceded his discharge, he refused an invitation to dine with the dictator in Porto Alegre, the Rio Grande do Sul state's capital city: "The guy killed my friends. I have a name to take care of. I could not condone such a monstrous human being."

Is the juego de posición Saldanha's legacy?

A closer look at the 1970 Brazilian team during its Mexican campaign demonstrates that Saldanha's footballing ideas permeated the Seleção's playing style across all six matches that led to the *tricampeonato*. I would even dare to say that some of his tactical understandings of the game have recently been implemented by Pep Guardiola's Manchester City and Hans-Dieter Flick's Bayern Munich.

Saldanha used to coin many catchphrases. As a media journalist, he knew how to use words not only to create great controversies with dictators, but also to summarize some complex concepts. During the 1970 World Cup qualifiers, as the media questioned him about his players' constant positional changes in the field, he coined a phrase that expressed his whole football philosophy: "A football field is not an allotment. Nobody owns a land portion, with a fixed position."

The 'false nine' played by Tostão is evidence of Saldanha's influence over the team. But the Seleção's fourth goal in the 1970 Final is the clearest example of the implementation of Saldanha's philosophy. This goal definitely has a strong influence in the *Juego de Posición* (positional play) employed by some of the most successful managers' current strategies in the top European football leagues.

Look up this goal on the internet. The play starts slowly, with Clodoaldo displaying some *jogo bonito* skills and dribbling past four Italians in Brazil's defensive field, before passing the ball to Rivelino, the left-winger, who was in defence, and advances to the midfield and makes a straight, long pass to Jairzinho. There, we start to see Saldanha's ideas in action—what was Jairzinho, a classic number 7, a right-winger, doing in the left-wing position? Clearly, Rivelino had retreated to the midfield so Jairzinho could occupy 'his land portion' in the field. Play goes on; Jairzinho cuts to the mid and after beating two Italians, delivers the ball to Pelé who, without hesitation, passes it to the right-wing space, which was emptied by Jairzinho's move to the left. Pelé knew that a *free man* (a key concept of positional play) would occupy that new 'vacant lot'. So, there was Carlos Alberto, the captain, moving at full speed from his right fullback position, to score a goal to seal the Jules Rimet trophy's destiny.

This fourth goal was scored in the 41st minute of the second half when Italy looked already beaten by the Brazilian team. It's worth mentioning that just a few moments before Carlos Alberto's goal, Brazil's TV official match narrator was announcing that Médici would make an official pronouncement to the nation as soon as the final whistle was blown.

That dad on whose lap that four-year-old boy celebrated the Seleção's *tricampeonato* was also born in *Alegrete*, Saldanha's hometown. Who knew that one day that boy would share the stories that his father was afraid to say, even to himself? After all, the walls had many ears during the dictatorship, and not everyone had a microphone to voice their ideas. But, big or small, *Alegrete's* voices left an enduring legacy in Brazil's football history.

CHAPTER 4

The Most Painful Defeat: The 1982 Sarrià Tragedy and the demise of the *jogo bonito*

'Not even the 7-1 hurt so much.' This has been the general feeling among Brazilians when comparing the 2014 humiliation to that defeat against Italy. It was the 1982 Spain World Cup. The Brazil national team, the Seleção, hadn't won anything since 1970. The pressure for the fourth world title was mounting. But the nearly unanimous mood in the country was that the Canarinhos[2] were fated to win the tournament.

Zico, Sócrates, Toninho Cerezo and Falcão in the midfield made up the Seleção's perfect magic square. Telê Santana, the master of the masters, was the team's manager. Brazil was slowly leaving a dictatorship. Democratic winds were blowing back in the country. The first elections for state governors since 1962 would take place later that year. Most importantly, three days earlier than the fateful match, the team had smashed Argentina, then world champions, in the same Sarrià Stadium. That 3-1 win not only avenged the Seleção's suspicious elimination from the 1978 World Cup; it was there that Junior, after scoring the goal that sent our hermanos

---

[2] *Canarinhos* (little canary bird) was another nickname for the Brazilian team. A few months before the tournament, the samba Fly, Canarinho was recorded by Junior, the team's left-back, becoming an instant hit and the team's soundtrack for that World Cup campaign. It's a positive and happy song that sings "Fly, Canarinho, fly - show to Spain what we already know" The Canarinho nickname wasn't used after the 1982 World Cup.

back home, celebrated with nice samba steps on the corner mark. His celebration was a signal to the world: the jogo bonito, the magic 'football-art' was back! But then the Seleção met Paolo Rossi ... and the rest is tragedy.

Brazilian football has produced memorable icons and stories. Brazil's national team has left lasting images of victory and bliss in the minds and souls of football fans across the world. Pelé conquering the 1958 title in Sweden as a teenager; or Garrincha, the 'joy of the people' using his bowlegs to win the 1962 World Cup nearly by himself, will remain forever as magnificent events in world footballing history. There is no real football fan who can forget the apex of the jogo bonito delivered by the 1970 Seleção—journalist and writer Philip Micallef considers the 1970 Brazilian squad as the "prototype of the total football system that was perfected by the Dutch throughout the 1970s". Players continually changing their positions, the 'false 9' enacted by Tostão and the attacking advances of defenders such as Carlos Alberto (who even scored a goal in the final match) are evidence that the 1970 Seleção has impacted football tactics way beyond their time.

Nevertheless, as much as their football feats are enormous—so are the Seleção dramas. Those have been delivered on the world stage. They are entrenched in Brazil's football soul as much as they are present in their rivals' continuous mockery of the Seleção's biggest defeats: the Maracanazo and the Mineirazo.

The well-known Maracanazo is the Seleção's eminent 1950 World Cup Final defeat against Uruguay in front of 200,000 spectators in the Maracanã Stadium. The name Maracanazo sounds like a Spanish word; the term was coined by the Uruguayans to scorn the Brazilians and their overconfident attitude before that match. It means an epic setback in the world's largest stadium. However, despite the enormous pain it has caused, Brazilians quickly overcame that downfall by ruling the international football scene in subsequent decades.

The most recent huge drama for the Seleção was the Mineirazo; the shameful 7-1 defeat to the Germans in the 2014 World Cup semi-final. As it occurred in the Mineirão Stadium, the Brazilians themselves quickly came up with this term. Yet, despite the shame brought to the Seleção by the Mineirazo—or Mineiratzen, a joke with the German language—it swiftly became a funny tale in Brazilian pubs and on the streets. As evidence of the social and cultural changes in the country, Brazilians usually say that they would rather lose by 7-1 on the football pitch but win by the same score in their educational systems—something that is unfortunately far away from becoming a reality.

That leaves us with the Sarrià Tragedy. This is the very real drama that never stops to haunt Brazilian football. I was a 16-year-old Brazilian high schooler living in São Paulo when it happened. Half of our school's football team had gathered at a friend's house to watch that match together. It was a national holiday—as it used to be when the Seleção played a World Cup match. My friend's mum had baked some cakes that we devoured during the match while his stressed dad couldn't control himself and smoked one cigarette after another. The memories afterwards are clear: we walked across the neighbourhood's streets in a straight line, performing a funeral march. Other boys joined us in this walk: nobody said a word. The gloomy atmosphere continued during the week: I can't remember any other time that my school was so silent than in the days following that defeat.

Why? What happened on that 5th of July in Barcelona? Why did it become such a tragedy for the Brazilian people? Moreover, why is that the 1982 team was still so adored and admired not only in Brazil, but also around the world, despite being stopped by an inferior squad in the tournament's quarter-finals?

These questions are part of a footballing conundrum. As I watched the 1982 World Cup matches over and over, I became even more convinced that if Zico, Sócrates and co. have never won a World Cup—then too bad for the World Cup. 1982 was the end of an era: at the end of that match, the world said goodbye to the jogo bonito as we knew it. The corporate boxes started to welcome the commodified spectacle of so-called modern football. Dreamers such as Telê and Sócrates would no longer have room in the new footballing order. But in 1982, they proved their worth and left their eternal mark in world footballing history.

A perfect crusade

The campaign that led to that quarter-final match against Italy was outstanding. Telê took over the team in February 1980, winning 24 times with 6 draws and only two defeats—one against the former USSR in 1980 and one against Uruguay in 1981. During this period, the Seleção scored 84 times and allowed 20 goals, with 14 clean sheets. Only once did the team fail to score a goal, and that was in a friendly against Chile in Santiago. The 1982 Brazilian team played superb attacking offensive football that fascinated the world. In his 1982 book, 'Brazil: The Glorious Failure', Stuart Horsfield affirmed that this team was the "most exhilarating and entertaining World Cup side ever".

The 1982 World Cup had a unique arrangement. It was the first time that 24 national teams were playing in the tournament's finals. In the first phase, these teams were split into six groups of four teams each; the best two would qualify for the next stage. Then, four groups of three teams were formed, and the winner of each group would play in the semi-finals.

Brazil beat USSR 2-1 in its first match of the competition; a tough battle where the Soviets scored the first goal but could not resist the Brazilians' attacking power. After the anxiety of the first match, the team went into cruise mode to beat Scotland 4-1 and New Zealand 4-0 to finish first in its group, with ten goals for, and only two against.

On the other hand, Italy had a completely disappointing first phase, drawing its three initial matches (Poland, 0-0; Peru, 1-1; Cameroon, 1-1) and only surviving in the tournament due to a one-goal-for lead over the African side. Paolo Rossi, who hadn't played competitive football in the prior two years, looked really unfit during these initial matches.

Brazil's group was completed by the Argentinian side, who began the tournament with a defeat (1-0) against Belgium but recovered in the following matches by beating Hungary (4-1) and El Salvador (2-0). Like Italy, they came second in their group.

Brazilians love to believe that their team was the best in this group, which might be true, as they had international names such as Zico, Sócrates, Falcão, Junior and Cerezzo. However, we cannot forget that the Italians also had great players, such as Conti, Tardelli and Gentile. Furthermore, the Argentinians had fabulous footballers too with names such as Kempes, Passarella and Diego Maradona, then a 22-year-old man who would win the following World Cup for the Argentinians, scoring some beauties—but also scoring one of the most controversial goals in football's history, with God's hand help (La Mano de Dios).

The group was placed in Barcelona with the winner moving to the World Cup semi-finals. In the first match at the Sarrià Stadium, Italy defeated the Argentinians

2-1 in front of 43,000 people. Tardelli and Cabrini scored for Italy and at the end of the match, Passarella left his mark for the South Americans.

After that contest, Brazilian midfielder Falcão called Bruno Conti to praise him for his performance against the Argentinian side. They were colleagues and friends at Italian side A.S. Roma and formed the incredible midfield who won the Scudetto (the Italian Cup) for the club in the 1980-81 and 1981-82 seasons, after waiting 40 years. Falcão, nicknamed the 'King of Rome' (the Divine) by Roma supporters, and Conti discussed when they should come back to the team after the World Cup. They wanted some holidays. In that phone call, Conti had the clear idea that he would come back to work earlier than his Brazilian colleague.

In the second match of the group, Brazil beat Argentina. It was a fantastic performance by the Seleção, who were winning 3-0 near the end of the game, when they lost their focus after Maradona kicked Batista's stomach in the 85th minute. Dieguito received a red card, but Diaz scored a final minute goal for the Argentinians.

As the Seleção had one goal-for advantage over the Italians in the group, they just needed a draw against the Azzurri to qualify for the semi-finals. That game would see a team that had scored 13 goals in the tournament and conceded just three playing a squad that had only scored four goals and had three scored against them.

An unforgettable match

As recently as March 2020, the influential Spanish football news outlet, *Marca*, ranked the 1982 Brazil vs Italy match as one of the top 50 games in football's history. Yet, Tim Lewis in a 2014 piece published by the *British Esquire* rates it as the "greatest game in World Cup history". He claims that this match changed not only football history, but also the lives of many who watched it. My high school teammates agree with Lewis: one friend recently told me that that match destroyed all his footballing dreams and that he will never overcome that pain.

It was a match where the Brazilian attack played the Italian defence. The Seleção's magic square swapped positions and roles, moving forward and pushing the Azzura's defence. Nevertheless, the Brazilians struggled to find any spaces in the fierce Italian defensive line. Gaetano Scirea, the Italian libero, constantly swept behind his defenders to protect Zoff's goalposts.

Surprisingly, it was the Italians who scored first and very early in the game. As in previous matches, the Brazilians took a while to wake up on the pitch. They were caught by Cabrini's cross that found Paolo Rossi totally unmarked behind Junior to score the first of what would be his hat-trick in the match.

Seven minutes and a few lost chances later, Sócrates found the equalizer, scoring after a wonderful assist from Zico. The world order was restabilised. But the fierce Italian defence, that saw Zico needing to change his jersey after it was torn by Gentile, put psychological pressure on the Brazilians. In the 25th minute, a rookie mistake by Cerezo left Paolo Rossi free in front of Waldir Peres, the Brazilian goalkeeper. Rossi did not miss that rare chance. Italy went into the break ahead 2-1.

In the end, a rigid tactical plan and a well-designed strategy won out over passion and freedom. A few say that Brazil played a 4:2:2:2 tactical formation, with Falcão and Cerezo being the holding midfielders, while Sócrates and Zico advanced to attack with Serginho and Éder. However, the positional changes were so constant and quick in that magic square that Falcão was always moving up to attack—he scored Brazil's second goal, which would have been the World Cup Final-qualifier if the Seleção knew how to stay put in the last 20 minutes to maintain the 2-2 scoreline and defend their one-goal-for advantage. Yet Telê refused to say anything to his team that would contradict his beliefs in the *jogo bonito*. Brazil kept advancing and looking lazy in defence. After a corner, as the ball was leaving the Brazilian box, all defenders moved up but one—Junior, the left back who had scored against Argentina. The Italian side put the ball back and it dropped at Paolo Rossi's fast feet, and he couldn't miss from such a short range. Junior raised his right arm, claiming an off-side position. However, it was he who had kept Rossi onside. The 1982 dream was over. The *Sarrià Tragedy* was sealed.

Even Spanish fans acknowledged that the 1982 Seleção were unique. As the team arrived at their hotel after the defeat, a few local fans waited for them, holding banners that read: "Fuerza Brazil! It's not always the best team that wins!". That team was so adored that Brazilian journalists were as depressed as the team after the loss. Usually, they were very quick to criticise any tiny Seleção mistakes in their match reports, but they did not say a critical word after the semi-final defeat at the 1982 World Cup. Instead, they offered comfort and solidarity to the players.

It took another 12 years for Brazil to win another World Cup after the *Sarrià Tragedy*. Yet, that 1994 side who won the US tournament was the antithesis of the 1982 team. Playing pragmatic, defensive football and managed by Parreira, a coach who once declared that "magic and dreams are finished in football", Romário's team only won the Cup in a penalty shootout against Italy—always them! However, if Baggio had scored his penalty and Romário had missed his, it would be the Italians, not the Brazilians, who would be in front in the World Cup title tally. A penalty is all that separates these two proud nations in football history.

In the past four decades, fans and journalists around the world have been asking the 1982 team's key players whether they would trade their *jogo bonito* style for a win in that Sarrià match. This is a deep and philosophical football question which has largely remained unanswered. However, a central actor in that drama offered a clue in a book he published 30 years after the tragedy. Paolo Rossi, the 1982 World Cup Golden Ball and Golden Boot winner, wrote the preface for Paulo Falcão's 2012 book and revealed that he regards the first goal against the Seleção in the semi-final match as the most important of his career. Significantly, Falcão was awarded the Silver Boot at the tournament, despite the Seleção not making the World Cup Final.

Yet the answer to arguably the most philosophical football question ever asked comes even before Rossi's preface in Falcão's book. It is written on the cover as the subtitle:

Brazil 82:
The team that lost the World Cup
and conquered the world.

CHAPTER 5

Higuita, El Loco: A Colombian hero and a game-changer

South Americans fondly remember the great *porteros* who made history for their countries and teams in the subcontinent. The football world and the Latino aficionados will never forget names such as Uruguayan Mazurkiewicz—who, despite being considered the world's best goalkeeper in the early 1970s, is mostly recalled for his participation in one of the greatest 'non-goals' in football's history during the 1970 Mexico World Cup: Pelé, without touching the ball, employed a body *ginga* (sway) to dribble him, but ended up missing the final kick to the empty net.

Another cherished South American goaltender is Argentinian Goycochea who played with Maradona in the 1990 World Cup runners-up campaign in Italy. The region also produced keepers like Paraguayan Chilavert and Brazilian Rogério Ceni, who both went above and beyond what used to be the ordinary 'handwork' in their positions. They regularly used their feet to score several free kicks and penalties for their teams.

Yet, as remarkable as all these men were both within and outside the penalty box, none can be considered as revolutionary as René Higuita. The Colombian goalkeeper is unique in the South American goalkeeping scene. I dare to suggest that Colombian football is undeniably marked by two eras: the 'before Higuita' and 'after Higuita' eras.

Many will say that this is an overstatement. After all, Higuita, as fantastic and dramatic as he was, cannot be compared to the 1990–1994 Colombian teams. That squad, despite not winning many titles, played with an unforgettable style and made significant history, including humiliating an arrogant Argentinian team with a 5-0 demolition at the Monumental de Núñez Estadio in Buenos Aires during a 1993 South American qualifier clash for the 1994 World Cup in the US. That win avenged the then recent Colombian defeat to Argentina in the penalty shootout at the 1993 *Copa America* semi-final. It generated memorable headlines across South America. On the Colombian side, the newspapers stamped their front pages with: *Monumental Colombia!* But in Argentina, the front pages of the main papers were totally black except for one word in capital letters: VERGÜENZA! (SHAME!).

Others may argue that Pablo Escobar's influence over Colombian football should mark historical periods. The ruthless and not-too-inspiring impact of the drug kingpin within the Colombian social and footballing landscape is remarkable, but it cannot be compared to Higuita's—*El Loco's* (The Madman's) legacy to the Colombian people. Why? Because Higuita, despite his many critics, was an inspiration to the *Paisa* kids—and nothing is stronger than a football dream.

So, as much as Valderrama's and Rincon's team played amazing football, bringing hope to the Colombian people and enchanting the football world during two World Cups in the 1990s, with Escobar leaving his bloodthirsty and corrupt brand across the country in the same period, Higuita left a superior and enduring vision within Colombian children's minds and hearts. He inspired them to dream to perform in the goalkeeping role that was once always destined for weaker kids. And what is football if not a game for dreamers?

It is important to highlight that Colombian society is strongly stratified by an extremely unequal social class system that started as soon as the Spanish colonizers arrived in the country in the late 1400s and early 1500s, and this system became official in 1994. People are formally ranked within six social classes according to a range of economic and social markers. Most of the lower social classes are made up of dark-skinned Colombians who have Indigenous or African ancestry. These populations receive social class numbers between one and three. The law assigns class numbers to housing, ensuring that different localities are populated according to their social class.

Most of the best football played in the country can be seen in the neighbourhoods of the lower social classes; it's on their irregular streets in the middle of slums or in poorly maintained schools and parks that most children run after a ball and kick it across this beautiful land. However, before Higuita, these dark-skinned children dreamt to play as midfielders, or to be the great striker who would redeem Colombian football and guide it to the pinnacles of world football. If you were not skilled enough, you would end up as a defender; but no child ever wanted to be a goalkeeper. Colombian children would rather play without a goalkeeper than be within the goalposts.

Higuita changed these children's feelings and world vision forever. After watching his heroic runs with the ball towards the opposition, his positioning as a sweeper to stop the other team's attack, after seeing him score several goals, and later witnessing *El Loco's* famous scorpion kick defence at Wembley—children all over the country dreamed of being the number 1. The player who would not only save the team with his hands but would also leave the penalty box with the ball at his feet, tricking opponents, acting as a playmaker and even scoring several goals from free kicks and penalty shots. Higuita was a Colombian football hero who inspired generations of poor kids to try and be better in what they loved to do.

Still, this footballing hero had also his low off-field moments that jeopardized his career. For example, in 1993 he was jailed for seven months for his participation in a kidnapping. He was the link between the kidnappers and the kidnapped person's family—delivering the ransom and receiving an award for his work. This jail time cost him his participation at the 1994 US World Cup.

Perhaps one of the most controversial episodes of Higuita's off-field life was when he visited Pablo Escobar in jail, playing a football match with him and other drug trafficking prisoners in *La Catedral* prison, the same penitentiary that was built by the capo. Despite Higuita's attempts to justify his visit over the years, many Colombians still state that it was the largest moral shock *El Loco* ever caused to them. However, at the end of the day, Higuita is a human hero—a man who was raised in a beautiful but violent country where it is often hard to see the blurred line that separates heroes from villains.

The raising of Higuita

Born in 1966 in a low social class area of Medellin's city, René Higuita was raised by his grandmother after his mum's passing when he was a young child. Early in his life, he worked several casual jobs to earn a basic living. His goalkeeping career started by chance; he was the school team's striker, but in a trial match where *Independiente Medellín* scouts came to watch and pick a few players for their team, the school team's goalkeeper was injured and Higuita was placed between the goalposts—and he never left. In 1985, he played for the Colombian U-19 team in the Paraguay South American championship, where he first displayed some of his tricks outside the penalty box that would become his future trademark.

In the same year, he signed his first professional contract with *Millonarios FC* in Bogotá. There, he consolidated his keeper-playmaker style, inheriting not only the 'El Loco' nickname from the club's veteran Argentinian keeper Alberto Vivalda, but also the boldness to leave his goal area unprotected to launch himself into the attack, dribbling opponents and carrying the ball to the midfield or even further.

In 1986, as a 20-year-old goalkeeper, Higuita went back to his home city to play for his beloved *Atlético Nacional de Medellín*. It was in the *Nacional* that he won his most prestigious titles, including bringing the *Copa Libertadores de America* trophy to Colombia for the first time in 1989. It was at *Atlético Nacional* under coach Francisco Maturana's leadership where he further developed his 'crazy' style and mastered his free-kick and penalty-shot techniques. You only need to watch his videos on the internet to realize that he genuinely was a goalkeeper-libero; he stood outside the box to cut off his opponent's attack and, as soon as he recovered the ball, he would try to advance with it to attack. At other moments, after a save and with the ball in his hands, he would roll the ball to himself and leave his area, moving the ball forward towards the midfield. There were plenty of times when angry opponents would be yellow- carded for their violent tackles on that long, dark, curly-haired goalkeeper who defied the game's 'natural' flow.

It is important to stress that, despite his outlandish playing style, Higuita was a solid goalkeeper who could perform amazing saves like the best glovemen of his era. As a professional player, he scored 43 goals, including 36 penalties, 6 free kicks and even one 'goalpost to goalpost' goal. Three of those goals were scored while serving the Colombian national team, for whom he played five *Copa Americas* (reaching third place in 1987 and 1995) and the 1990 World Cup, with a total of 68 caps as the team's first-choice keeper.

Higuita's teammates usually adjusted to his style, so as soon as he left the box to try his attacking moves, a few defenders stayed behind to protect the goal area. Nevertheless, his attacking advances were not always successful, as witnessed by the entire football world at the 1990 World Cup in Italy.

Colombia was only in its second-ever World Cup Finals' campaign, and for the first time had reached the round of 16. Playing an exhilarating style, the South Americans would face the Cameroon team in a knock-out match that promised to be exciting, as the 'Indomitable Lions' were the other sensation of the tournament. Seated on the Cameroonians' bench was the legendary and veteran striker Roger Milla, then playing in France for Montpellier, where he lined up in the attack with Valderrama, the Colombian's captain.

The 50,000 fans who packed the *Stadio San Paolo* in Naples had to wait till the second half of extra time to see a goal. It was only in the 106th minute that Milla scored for the Africans. Then, just three minutes later, Higuita's so-called major fail happened: as Colombia rushed to attack looking for the equalizer, the Cameroon team retreated with their whole team in their defensive half. Then the ball was kicked back to Colombia's half, where *El Loco*, practically by himself, was already positioned as a libero, passing it to a defender who was coming back to support him. At that moment, Milla quickly approached the defender. Perceiving the danger, Higuita signalled to his teammate to kick the ball to the other side; however, instead of following the keeper's instructions, the defender delivered a crooked pass back to Higuita that went behind him. Noticing that Higuita was in trouble, Milla sped up and took it from the keeper's feet, rushing towards the empty South American goal, sealing Cameroon's World Cup fortunes. The Colombians would still score one goal before the final whistle, but they ran out of time to equalize, and the Lions went through to the next stage of the tournament.

Blaming Higuita for Milla's decisive second goal is practically unanimous worldwide. After all, in 1990 he was an eccentric goalkeeper who dared to challenge the keeper's traditional role, playing in a line-up of Indigenous and black players with long hair. Yet, a closer analysis of his actions tells a different story: his defender should never have passed back to him, as Milla and other Cameroonians were already rushing towards them. And if the pass, instead of going behind him, went to his front, Higuita would have had time to advance with the ball or at least kick it forward. Another relevant point is that Milla already knew about Higuita's impressive style through Valderrama, his teammate at Montpellier. Thus, the experienced striker would have planned some sort of pressing attack towards him if an opportunity arose.

Nevertheless, Higuita's critical 'mistake' was not enough to erase his influence over the game. Despite the blame he carried for this defeat, his playing style on Italian fields had already left a profound mark in some football-thinking heads during the World Cup. It would soon provoke a deep change in football.

La Ley Higuita and the emergence of the sweeper keeper

Higuita's impact on his national soil is a fact and he continues to be relevant in Colombian football today, broadcasting his opinions via several well-followed social media channels. However, it is also important to state his influence over a significant change in the game beyond Colombia. *El Loco's* playing style has strongly influenced the evolution of the goalkeeper position over the past three decades. Now we can enjoy magnificent keepers such as Neuer, Ederson and Allyson playing outside their box like central-defenders, or as goalkeeper-liberos; Guardiola, Sampaoli and other top coaches choose their shot-stoppers not only for their ability to produce miraculous saves, but also for their capacity to read the game beyond their own goalposts. They use their feet to make accurate passes and generate attacking opportunities for their teams. All of this is due to Higuita's creative performances during the 1990 World Cup.

In Higuita's era, it was rare to see a goalkeeper with sufficient skills on their feet, and enough audacity to leave their area and attempt any play that would push their team to attack. Keepers would usually put the ball back in play with a big kick, either from a goal kick, or, after a save or a pass back, just throw the ball from their hands to their foot and try to kick it as far as they could into the opposition's half. However, at the 1990 World Cup in Italy, Higuita surprised the football world with his challenging and now legendary out-of-position plays where he acted as a play-maker for the Colombian team—not always successfully, as we have seen. He was the first keeper to challenge the goalkeeper's defensive *status quo* in the world football's top event.

His unique, risky and original performances in Italy prompted an intense debate within football circles about the necessity to improve keepers' feet games. As the 1990 World Cup was marked by an incredibly low goal average (2.2 goals/match, a record low that still stands), football officials saw the sweeper-keeper style as an exceptional chance to increase the speed of the game, thus increasing goal-scoring opportunities and football's attractiveness to new audiences, particularly to United States viewers where the next World Cup was scheduled to take place.

In the same year, during world football's technical conference held after the 1990 World Cup at the *Centro Tecnico Federale di Coverciano*—the Italian Football Federation headquarters in Florence—the back pass rule was determined, and it was implemented at the 1992 Barcelona Olympic Games. Before this rule—that prevents goalkeepers from retrieving a teammate's foot pass with their hands—many teams who were winning a match used to waste time (and bore spectators) with an endless passing game between defenders and keepers who could just catch the ball with their hands at the first sign of an attacker. *La Ley Higuita* (the back-pass rule) not only ended this tedious practice, but it also sowed the football imagination of coaches who started to use the high-pressure strategy on the full field to quickly recover the ball, transforming the game's speed and attractiveness.

There are not many players in football history like *El Loco*; players whose innovative and tactical styles to position a team and play the game have actually changed football's laws. Higuita has had an enduring impact on the way we now enjoy, understand and play football. After the implementation of the back-pass rule, Higuita rightly said that he changed football in a way that Pelé, Messi or Maradona never did.

CHAPTER 6
Azul y Oro, Maradona *y* Riquelme: Power, neoliberalism and passion in *La Bombonera*

Setting foot in Buenos Aires after an absence of more than two decades certainly inspired relevant memories, but also many more surprises. Even the most incidental observer who has not visited the once-beautiful Argentine capital in a while would be shocked—not only by the extent of the poverty on the city's streets, but also by the decay of its architecture. What was once known as the 'Paris of South America' has clearly struggled to preserve its historical buildings. It is impossible to walk around its streets without sensing the prolific urban deterioration caused mainly by the implementation of neoliberal policies across the country.

However, as I explored the city further, I discovered Buenos Aires still deserves the title of the world's most passionate football city. Its stadiums are part of what transformed this city into a 'football paradise'. Contrary to most cities in the world where teams train and play in public venues, Buenos Aires football has retained a unique British tradition—only comparable to Montevideo and London—where nearly every club must have its own stadium, regardless of the dimensions. Hence, Buenos Aires is home to 36 football stadiums, each with a capacity for more than 10,000 spectators, including world-famous arenas where epic games have taken place and football history has been written, like *La Bombonera* and *El Monumental de Núñez*. Most importantly, there are countless small-sized football stadiums spread across the city in which Buenos Aires' communities proudly display their heritage to further build familial and social bonds by evoking the grandeur of their past.

Embodied by its stadiums and embedded in the city's social life, Argentinian football is a true ritual that becomes more intense throughout Buenos Aires' weekends. A walkabout during a Saturday afternoon around the capital's neighbourhoods reveals that football is the chief symbolic instrument connecting the people of Buenos Aires both socially and historically Their *carnivalesque* performances, combined with their hyperbolic football communications (that many times include violent clashes between groups of supporters for opposing teams—the *Barra Bravas*), tell past and present rivalries and struggles for social and political hegemony that go far beyond the fields. Passion, social class clashes, local disputes, as well as state and even national political power are at stake when the *porteños* (as Buenos Aires' inhabitants are known) march across the city's streets towards their stadiums to support their teams.

The supporters' (*hinchas*) parades and their subsequent performances within the stadiums both carry and construct a range of social values. They promote strict codes of hegemonic masculinity where a specific type of bodily expression is considered at the top of the gender hierarchy: a body that can hold the pressure of other bodies, a strong body that challenges (even violently) other bodies, and, most importantly, a body who never gives up on their club. This is the Argentinian *aguante*—a concept that mixes mighty and huge bodies with honour, loyalty and passion for the club above all. Whilst the *hinchas'* performances maintain a rigid gender hierarchy, they can also suspend other social hierarchies, and suddenly, the ones who were in the margins (the poor) become the central part of the ritual and may question the dominant social order.

Argentina can be perceived as a peripheral country in terms of the world's economic order, but it is a significant and respected realm when it comes to football's 'concert of nations'. Thus, the fans who can be seen in the streets of the *La Boca* neighbourhood—an impoverished working-class district in Buenos Aires—embody the social clash between tradition and neoliberalism in both Argentinian football and society; a struggle that confirms its intensity and dynamism when football parades end up at the world-renowned *La Bombonera*, Boca Juniors' sacred stadium. The clash further comes to life when we look at the history of two Argentinian football idols: Diego Armando Maradona and Juan Román Riquelme. More on that later in this chapter.

JORGE KNIJNIK

Boca Juniors: Local passion, global brand, and political powerhouse

Boca Juniors is arguably the leading club in Argentinian football. Recent polls indicate that around 40% of Argentina's *hinchas* follow Boca. The club is also the most victorious club in Argentine football, followed closely by its major local rival, River Plate, with whom it stars in one of the world's most fervent derbies, *El Superclásico*. Boca Juniors (or simply 'Boca' as everyone refers to the club) is also one of the major winners in South American football: it holds six *Copa Libertadores de America* titles (the South American Champions League), which is just one title short of *Independiente,* another Argentinian club that has not won a title since 1984. Boca also holds three Intercontinental Cup titles, the former challenge between the South American and European champions, which was replaced by the FIFA Club World Cup in 2005.

Boca Juniors was established in 1905 by five Italian migrants. Since its inception at the start of the last century, the club has been associated with working-class people and poor national and overseas migrants. Throughout its history, Boca has thrived based on its strong and passionate paying membership, its volunteers who run the club from top to bottom and its numerous followers across Argentina and beyond. The *Bosteros, Xeneizes* or *Boquenses* (as Boca's fans are known in Spanish) are bearers of the club's traditions and histories that have passed from one generation to another.

Nowadays, Boca Juniors is a global brand. Since the early 2000s, the club has diversified its marketing strategies and it currently has around 1,000 licensed products; from the traditional club headscarves and jerseys, to pens and notebooks and even an agreement with major international brand Warner Bros that sees the famous Bugs Bunny character wearing Boca's apparel in typical *Boquense* fashion. Its matches are broadcast to audiences across the world, reaching around 45 million people from countries such as China and Japan, but also attracting North American spectators, mostly in Los Angeles, Miami, and New York, and in Mexico, where Boca has its biggest overseas fan club. Boca usually takes advantage of the Southern Hemisphere winter and the associated breaks in the

Argentinian football calendar to tour abroad to further develop its relationship with its overseas followers.

The club has also built a museum (*Museo de la Pasión Boquense*, or the 'Museum of the Boca's supporter passion') that is one of the major cultural attractions in Buenos Aires, charming thousands of national and international tourists. An exclusive Boca truck travels the country to sell the club's merchandise to *Boquenses* spread around Argentina, while a customized fleet of taxis helps supporters to travel within Argentina's biggest cities. Fanatic Boca *hinchas* can hold their passion to their graves, as Boca even has its own cemetery.

All these marketing achievements didn't come easily to the club. They faced resistance from their 'true fans', which exposes the continuous paradoxes embedded in the club's process of modernization. It began in the mid-1990s and was aligned with the neoliberal forces that control international football and pushed for new 'FIFA standards' to make the game a global power. Since then, Boca has embarked on a new era where a group of young and fresh businessmen, led by engineer and entrepreneur Mauricio Macri, took over Boca's board and presidency. The main slogan of Macri's group was "to recover the missed glory". Elected in 1995 with the support of relevant Argentinian millionaires in an alliance with veteran high-class Boca fans, Macri was re-elected another two times (in 1999 and 2003). Being Boca's president also propelled his political career: he was subsequently elected Buenos Aires' Mayor in 2007, re-elected in 2011 and finally became Argentina's President in 2015.

Macri's terms at the top of Boca can be summarized by modern sports management procedures that aimed to improve the club's financial position. They were successful and also brought Boca back to a winning football streak after years of disillusionment. However, as the marketing department took over every single aspect of the club, many traditional *hinchas* felt alienated in the process. Treated no more as members and co-owners of the club, but as mere customers, they boisterously protested that Boca was losing its soul. A clear example of this struggle between traditional and neoliberal practices happened in 1998 when Nike, just two years after becoming Boca's sponsor and sporting gear supplier, decided to change the club's jersey technology and implement a few tweaks on its design.

JORGE KNIJNIK

The *azul y oro* controversy

In 1910, the *azul y oro* (blue and gold) Boca jersey's colours were decided by a group of *La Boca* inhabitants who, after a few meetings without reaching a consensus, decided to follow Juan Brichetto's suggestion. As this *Boquense* and Italian immigrant's job was to authorize all ships entering the city's port, his proposal was that the club should follow the flag colours of the next vessel to arrive in the dockyards. A Swedish freighter was the 'winner' of this selective process, and since then, with just a few design changes, the club has worn its traditional blue jersey with a wide horizontal, golden stripe. This jersey is a powerful sign to the Boca *hinchas*, who believe that opponents fear the jerseys' historical weight, and that often the team wins games just by wearing it (*'les ganamos con la camiseta'*).

Despite this strong connection, Nike wanted to introduce a dry-fit technology in the club's jersey in 1998. This innovative technology would control moisture, provide better airing for the players and eliminate sweat. It would also be appealing to a fan who could go out after 90 minutes of jumping non-stop in the stands without smelling of sweat.

Nike did not account for the fans' reaction to the non-sweating jersey. A key concept of Argentinian football is *garra*—a combination of physical fight, spirit, determination and moral effort symbolized by sweat—and even blood—in a player's shirt. The Boca *hinchas*, when angry with the team after a poor performance, have a chant where they sing: "*La camiseta de Boca se tiene que transpirar*" ("One must perspire the Boca's jersey"). How would a player make his *garra* evident after a match if the new jersey would not allow him to show he left everything on the ground?

Then Senator and former Buenos Aires State Governor, Antonio Cafiero, who served in high government echelons under Peron's administration, wrote a protest letter to the *Clarín*, the main Argentinian newspaper. Cafiero claimed that the *hinchas* wanted to see the players "soaked in sweat. We do not want our team in a dispassionate, postmodern, and anti-perspiration costume."

The story of the 'dry-fit' jersey is an example, among many others, of how tradition and modernity coexist and clash within Boca's everyday life. The political struggles between passion and management *(pasión y gestión,* as per Mauricio Macri's book title) and the tensions and paradoxes between community history and neoliberal measures are also represented in the histories of its two major footballing icons: Diego Armando Maradona and Juan Román Riquelme.

El Diez

The passing of Diego Maradona on November 25, 2020, stopped the football world—and beyond. The scenes of millions of Argentinians challenging the COVID-19 pandemic restrictions to go onto Buenos Aires' streets to pay a final tribute to their idol were heartbreaking. Supporters of archrival clubs such as River Plate and Boca Juniors forgot their historic and bitter hostilities to embrace each other while mourning the death of their football myth. Around the world, most major newspapers highlighted Maradona's passing in their front-page headlines. Celebrities from the sporting and art worlds expressed their grief and admiration for '*El Pibe de Oro'* ('the Golden Boy', one of Maradona's nicknames that refers to an old Argentinian tango telling the story of a poor boy who, through football, steps up the social ladder towards consecration). Major sporting leagues such as the English Premier League, and even the famous All Blacks, the New Zealand rugby team, paid their last respects to a player considered by many as 'the best to have ever laid his feet on a football field'.

French President Emmanuel Macron wrote a eulogy in which he declared his admiration for Maradona as a footballer, acknowledging his central role in "the most geopolitical football match in history". He was referring to the 1986 clash between Argentina and England at the Mexico World Cup, where according to him, Maradona performed both good and evil in the same match, scoring the two "paramount and famous goals in football history". The French leader also took the opportunity to slightly pick on France's historical rivals across the English Channel.

Diego Armando Maradona, also known as *'El Diez'* ('the Ten'), was always a rebel within the football world. However, unlike other sports celebrities, his rebellious attitude had either specific targets or were for social causes. In his early days, he had a heated argument with principal Argentinian newspaper, the *Clarín,* whose journalists were severely critical of both him and the national team after their defeat in the 1982 Spain World Cup. Before the start of the 1986 Mexico World Cup and his starring performances there, Maradona was the only player to publicly complain about the tournament's match scheduling. To comply with FIFA's commercial TV agreements, which were mainly aimed at the European market, the players were heavily exposed to high temperatures. The games were played in Mexican cities over 2,000 meters above sea level during peak heat hours.

Over the years, he cultivated the animosity of the all-powerful FIFA's former president João Havelange, who chaired the leading football body from 1974 to 1998, as well as the rancour of FIFA's then general secretary (and later FIFA's president) Joseph Blatter. Maradona paid a high price during his career for opposing these powerful football leaders. He felt vindicated when the FBI raided the 2015 FIFA congress in Zurich to put several high officers of the international sporting body in jail.

Nevertheless, *La Mano de Dios* (the hand of God) goal perhaps is the most relevant of Maradona's many revenges during his remarkable career. The Argentinians felt humiliated by England in the Malvinas (or Falklands) Islands War. Their wounded patriotism was still strong when the two teams faced each other in the 1986 World Cup quarter-finals. Maradona's scoring in a controversial manner and then, just five minutes later, notching the most incredible goal in World Cup history to beat the English team transformed him into more than an idol in his home country: for many, he became D10S—a wordplay with the Spanish word for God (*Dios*) and Maradona's number 10 jersey.

Maradona performed impressively, not only against England, but across the whole 1986 World Cup tournament. His solo displays of talent were the final piece of evidence that he embodied all the qualities that the Argentinian masses see in their everyday lives: malice, some sort of cheating, but also cunning and untamed passion. His talents, combined with his political views that made him close to left-wing Latin American leaders such as Fidel Castro, Hugo Chávez and Evo Morales, transformed Maradona into the most popular Argentinian archetype: a fervent man who never minced his words, and who lived intensely through the ups and downs of his passions, both on and off football pitches. Maradona was the personification of a tango.

In 2001, the Argentinian Football Federation (AFA) organized the National team's festive farewell match for Maradona. *El Diez* played one half with the *Albiceleste* Argentinian team jersey, and the second half with Boca's number 10 jersey where the name of his successor on the field could be read below the digits: *Román*. Many thought that the prototype Argentinian persona embodied by Maradona would also suit Román Riquelme. After all, he had already started to excite the Boca's *hinchas* not only with his midfield magic, but also for confronting some in the Boca Juniors' board.

Juan Román Riquelme, the next Boca number 10, was also a terrific midfielder who conquered the hearts of the *Boquenses*. However, unlike the myth he replaced, he was never an easy-to-define man. Behind the facade of the simplicity of his manners as a kid from a poor neighbourhood, there is a man who has two personas—the one that is exposed, and the one that hides behind the walls of his privacy.

El 10

Juan Román Riquelme, also known as '*El Torero*' ('The Bullfighter') is considered the most important player in Boca Junior's history. He arrived at the club as a 17-year-old whose only dream was to play at *La Bombonera*. After 18 years, he became not only the record-holder for most matches played at Boca's stadium, but also one of the club's most victorious players with 11 titles, including an Intercontinental Cup against Real Madrid in Tokyo (2000), and 3 *Copa Libertadores*, the super-hard and most adored competition among the *Boquenses*. According to him, one *Copa Libertadores* is worth ten titles for the Boca's *hinchas*. Riquelme also won the 1997 FIFA U-20 World Cup and the 2008 Beijing Olympics with the national team, wearing the famous *Albiceleste* jersey. *El Torero* also holds several individual accolades, such as being a four-time 'Argentinian Footballer of the Year' and twice the *Copa Libertadores'* most valuable player.

Recognized for his strong personality, Riquelme was perceived by his colleagues as the 'king of the change room'. He could silence a teammate just by gazing at them, without saying a word. However, he would never criticize a teammate in public, leaving the hard conversations to be had behind the scenes. He always displayed leadership skills, and many co-players would see him as a coach on the field; Riquelme would defy his coach's instructions if he felt it was necessary and command his team to play the way he wanted.

His imposing and sometimes rebellious temperament resulted in several clashes with Boca's football authorities. One of these battles earned him the 'Topo Gigio' nickname that has stuck with him. In 2001, *El Torero* was involved in a major dispute with Boca's board who wanted to sell him to FC Barcelona, as the Buenos Aires club was facing severe financial hardship. During this quarrel, Mauricio Macri, Boca's then president, leaked Riquelme's wages to the press in a bid to push him to accept the international deal which would bring some cash relief to the club. In the subsequent *Superclásico,* as he scored the second goal of Boca's 3–0 win at *La Bombonera, El Torero* didn't celebrate with his teammates: surprisingly, he ran towards the midfield to stop in front of Boca authorities' corporate box, where he provocatively placed his hands behind his ears, as if to say, 'leak something else now!' The following day, his protest gesture made the headlines of every Argentinian newspaper.

As with many Argentinian players who rose to stardom, Riquelme's origins are humble. The eldest in an 11-sibling family, at a young age he decided to leave school to pursue a playing career. His father agreed with his plans but imposed one condition: he must put his soul into his training, and Riquelme followed his advice. He was coached by his father in tough playing conditions that included constant rough games and damaged surfaces. It was in these settings that he learned how to endure any type of challenge from the hardest opponents across South America and the world.

It was also where he developed a unique playing style, employing a different tempo in his plays. A few people defined him as an old-style player, apparently too slow for modern football. However, as Jorge Valdano used to say, he was mentally faster. He could see not only what was happening on the field, but what would happen many moments later, and as a result he placed the ball wherever he wanted. He would appear to be walking on the field, just passing the ball to the side with no intention to attack, and then suddenly change the rhythm and start an in-depth play that would catch his opponents half-cocked. He also mastered the art of hiding the ball so well that his opponents could never steal it from his feet, and as they tried, Riquelme would 'nutmeg' them (kick the ball between the player's legs), causing a roar of ecstasy throughout the stadium.

For many analysts, this playing style was the foundation of Riquelme's football philosophy. It can be argued that *El Torero* was the intellectual owner of the teams he played for—these sides basically gravitated around him. For Boca's fans, he was their idol. In 2014, when he could not reach a contractual agreement to stay at the club, he decided to go back and play for Argentino Juniors, his first professional club and where he would retire a year later after helping the club to be promoted to the Argentinian championship's first tier. In that year, many *Boquenses* started to attend Argentino Juniors' matches just to follow their idol for the pleasure of watching him on the field.

Riquelme has always seen himself as a passionate *Boquense*—someone who played for the *hinchas*, not for the board, nor for the money. He would never play for archrivals River Plate, even if they offered him the best contractual conditions: if he sported that red and white jersey, he would not be allowed to enter his family's home anymore. When he retired, many asked him if he would become Boca's manager, but being a football coach was not in his plans. However, without giving a straightforward response, he left the prospect of one day becoming Boca's president up in the air. It is a trajectory he has already started, as in 2019 he became the club's vice-president and four years later, he was elected as President defeating former President of Boca and Argentina, Mauricio Macri. Riquelme's answer about his professional future clearly mimicked his playing style—one of disguise, a classical ballet that used different tempos to overcome closed defensive lines and open room for his team's goals.

After Maradona's retirement, nobody could ever be designated as 'El Diez', so the *hinchas* started to call Riquelme 'El 10'. Two football prodigies, two Argentinian idols who, due to their footballing and personal features, represent the two sides of an ongoing battle between communal ideals and neoliberal ideologies within Boca and the broader Argentinian society.

The last tango in Buenos Aires

Maradona and Riquelme shared the playing field in an official match for the first and only time on 24 August 1997, when Boca won 2–1 against Argentino Juniors at

La Bombonera. On that night, D10S was wearing the number 10, while a young Riquelme wore the number 9. Both exhibited their talent to the Boca *hinchas* while talking to each other in the language of the football geniuses. A few months later, on 25 October 1997, Maradona played his last professional match at *El Monumental*. Wearing the number 10, Maradona left the field at half-time to be replaced by Riquelme wearing the number 20, and he helped Boca beat River 2–1.

In 2005, as Maradona starred in one of his many resurrections as the host of the TV show *La Noche del Diez* ('The night of Diez'), Riquelme was one of his most celebrated interviewees. In 2008, Maradona was in Beijing and kissed Riquelme in a typical Argentinian fashion when the *Albiceleste* received the gold medal at the summer Olympics.

These are just examples of the many bonds that connected Maradona and Riquelme. However, in late 2008, as Maradona stepped in as the national team coach, these ties collapsed; they were no longer dancing to the same song. There are many versions of why and how the bridges between Boca's idols eroded; some say that Maradona should have spoken with greater care when publicly discussing his plans regarding Riquelme's role in the national team; others say that *El Torero* could have given more leeway to *El Pibe de Oro*, instead of trying to control the team's change room. Yet, if they had done as people suggested, they simply would not be Maradona nor Riquelme anymore.

The public facts are that Riquelme did not accept Maradona's tactical plans for him. He went as far as saying that their ideas were not compatible and hence, they could never work together. Expressing his sadness, Riquelme retired from the national team. Conversely, Maradona was adamant that if a player refused to wear the *Albiceleste* jersey, he should never again be selected for the team. The pair never spoke to each other again. In Boca's 2019 elections, Maradona supported the former club president Daniel Angelici's group, voicing his discontent that *El Torero* sold himself for a few dollars. Riquelme was silently elected as the second vice-president under the opposition group led by Jorge Amor Ameal.

Perhaps both were right. They might have been as irreconcilable as the tradition versus modernity strain that has been stretching Boca in recent decades. While Maradona was amazing the world with his unstoppable dribbling, Riquelme was thinking how to manage the game; as Maradona displayed all his footballing instincts and used 'the hand of God' to win a World Cup, Riquelme was carefully calculating the space between defenders to deliver an impeccable assist; as Maradona, the short and quick man, implemented an incredibly fast pace on the field with his unpredictable runs, the tall Riquelme controlled the tempo of the ball, the game and everybody around him. As Maradona continued to publicly expose his spirit, dreams and personal failures in his post-football life, Riquelme decided to keep a low-profile, going under the radar and spending his days as a discreet family man and working backstage at the club he loves.

Nonetheless, beyond a clash of personalities, the Maradona versus Riquelme situation personified a broader struggle between community versus capital, public versus private, traditional versus neoliberal practices. While Maradona will be an eternal and ethereal myth for the Argentinian people, Riquelme has more concrete plans to build his golden path to the presidential chair of the club he adores—a club that has already shown how influential footballers can be in the political arena of the country.

Maradona will always represent the tradition and the passionate *hincha* on the stands; Riquelme, in contrast, has adjusted himself to the modern football world of the elites and, wearing his well-cut suits, personifies the new neoliberal times.

Yet, the actual Boca *hincha* does not have to choose between their two idols: a *Boquense* heart is large enough to entertain both the blue Maradona with his untamed tango steps, and gold Riquelme's disciplined ballet movements; that is why *azul y oro* (blue & Gold') come together as the *hinchada* sings to encourage Maradona while simultaneously presenting an enormous panel with Riquelme's face. In this sense, the Boca *hinchas* will continue their tradition of challenging neoliberal football and its gatekeepers as they shake *La Bombonera's* stands. After all, as the lyrics of their main chant (*"hinchada es una sola"*) say: the Boca's *hinchada* is one indivisible corpus who dances together, the only one that matters; the rest are bollocks.

The Maradona versus Riquelme affair shows how football possibly explains contemporary life in Argentina. However, for the Argentinian people, football and its idols are larger than life.

PART 2:
REVOLUTION

CHAPTER 7

The *Karimachus*: Bolivian women and the feminist battle in South American Football

'Si Me Permiten Hablar' is one of the most printed, reprinted, translated and commented-on Bolivian manuscripts of all time. Penned by Moema Libera Viezzer, a Brazilian feminist and sociologist, it was first published in 1977. Translated in English as '*Let Me Speak! Testimony of Domitila, a Woman of the Bolivian Mines*', the book conveys the strong, forthright and intense testimony of Domitila Barrios de Chungara, a Bolivian mining worker's wife.

In 1975, Domitila travelled to Mexico City to participate in the initial World Conference on Women. This was the first time that the United Nations convened a major meeting with a sole focus on women. It was attended by female lawyers, academics, teachers and other professionals from around the world. Despite being working-class, Domitila was not unsettled by all the middle-class, educated women as she walked on stage and took the microphone to deliver her speech. On the contrary, Domitila questioned all the feminist leaders seated in the audience, including North American activist Betty Friedan. She disconcerted these women by interrogating the dubious alliance among them. She asked what type of equality they were looking for, as she considered that they were so different, even though they all called themselves 'women'.

With her powerful words, Domitila was delivering an important message that shows there are other issues—larger than anatomy—that can unite or divide people. Four decades ago, issues such as social class, working conditions and ethnicity were already on her agenda. In this chapter, I trace an analogy between Domitila's life experiences of being oppressed and 'shushed' (but finding words to push back and be heard) and the lives of Bolivia's female footballers. Echoing Domitila's battles, I show how Bolivian women footballers, the *karimachus*, stood up, and using their collective voice, screamed: *"Let us play!"*

In 2018, FIFA's new guidelines forced clubs around the world to develop women's football teams to earn the right to be part of national and international competitions. Bolivian departmental (state) women's leagues were quickly set up to avoid FIFA and CONMEBOL sanctions. However, as they were rushed arrangements, there were many unplanned aspects. Clubs opened their doors for the women's game—but with no infrastructure whatsoever for them to play; no available facilities, no fields, and no consideration of players' age groups. Examples of this lack of protection for adolescent girls in their initial career steps are abundant: in 2022 in the Bolivian women's league, there was only one all-ages group. A few years ago, in 2019, a match in La Paz registered a 13-year-old girl playing with and against adults in their late 20s.

While the official records indicate that the Bolivian women's national team had its first international match as recently as 2019, other historical accounts show evidence that the initial Bolivian women's football league was created in the early 1990s. Furthermore, newspapers from the early 1980s have photographs of women's teams playing under a range of different circumstances, including on improvised pitches close to the mines. However, as there is no official documentation of these matches available, football historians are still digging for more evidence.

The karimachus or the Bolivian tomboys

One example of these 'invisible women' is Zdenscka Bacarreza, a past player and manager of the Bolivian women's football team. As a talented young girl who enjoyed her football, Bacarreza had to disguise herself as a boy to be allowed to step onto a football pitch. She even made up a boy's name (Marco Antonio) for herself to avoid punishment and further ejections from the game she loved. Concealing her identity was also a clever strategy to circumvent the inevitable criticism that Bolivian communities, even in the more urbanized places such as La Paz, would throw at her. A girl's place wasn't on a football pitch in a conservative and gender-rigid society such as Bolivia.

Like many other South American countries, Bolivia still largely embraces an orthodox gender ideology where female and male roles seem to be fixed and not open to questioning. According to these conventions, women belong in the private space of their homes doing the usual domestic chores: mothering, taking care of the elder members of the family, cleaning, washing, and cooking. *Karimachu* is the Quechua word (Quechua is one of the main Indigenous languages still spoken by approximately 10 million people of different ethnicities in South America) attributed to the women who dare to challenge the conservative gender norms. Initially used to designate effeminate men, the term was later used to describe homosexual women who did not follow the established gender order. Even though there are more than 30 spoken native languages in Bolivia, the *karimachu* term seems to be universal in the country. Hence, Bolivian women footballers quickly became accustomed to being known as '*karimachus*'.

Shamed by their families, ostracized by their communities, and stigmatized as being masculine and homosexual, the *karimachus* have endured several official and unofficial barriers just to play football, as have many other women across South America. During the 1990s, players such as Bacarreza could not compete in regular tournaments, nor be part of a national team, as the Bolivian football authorities demanded they be part of a local association to play football—however, local associations did not even exist in most of the Bolivian cities!

Nonetheless, the *karimachus* never gave up. They kept playing football, dreaming of one day being part of something better like being called up for a national squad and even playing in an international tournament. Their challenges were enormous, but their will was even bigger. Their accomplishments certainly go beyond the football pitch. They have made positive and enduring changes to Bolivian society. The pioneers of the Bolivian women's game have helped to redefine the concept of femininity in the country, including the role of women. The *karimachus* have transformed how women footballers are perceived in their communities; from 'perverted' lesbians to strong women. They have paved the way for new generations of Bolivian players.

Dejanos jugar!

Nowadays, the Bolivian *karimachus* are part of a larger footballing feminist struggle on the continent. Like Domitila, the feminist mining unionist who sought to be heard, the *karimachus* demand that Bolivian and other South American female footballers be free to play without any more legal, financial, or societal restrictions. The *karimachus'* footballing feminism aims to look after its communities and people. They want to play to improve the living conditions of their communities—particularly those of young women.

The *karimachus*' cry *Let us play!* (*Dejanos jugar!* in Spanish) is not an empty call, but a pledge for communal human rights that goes far beyond the football arena. It is a motto demanding that every single woman, irrespective of their social and cultural upbringing, or sexual orientation, can be involved in this vital component of every Bolivian and South American community: the game of football. The *karimachus* are the force behind the emerging feminist football movement on the continent.

CHAPTER 8

Smashing the Rules: Afonsinho and the end of players' slavery

Jean-Marc Bosman is well-known as being the first player in a major European league to challenge the draconian transfer rules that players were submitted to until the mid-1990s. His judicial challenge against RFC Liege—branded as the 'Bosman ruling'—ended the era where players were bound to their clubs even after the end of their contracts. When Bosman won his court case, UEFA was forced to change contractual rules which stated that players could only move between clubs if their former teams received a transfer fee. After 1995, players were free not only to move to another club after their contract expired, but also to sign a pre-contract agreement with another club if their existing contract had no more than six months remaining.

A few decades prior to the Bosman case, a South American player fought to break his obligations with his club. Afonsinho was the first player in Brazilian professional football to challenge the *lei do passe* (the license law). The *passe* was the player's authorization or permit to play. The *lei do passe* stated that clubs owned their players, regardless of whether they had a valid contract with them or not. To leave a club during or after a contract, another club had to literally buy the player, thus becoming the owner of the player's permit (*passe*) to play.

Established in 1964, the *lei do passe* was so harsh on players that clubs did not have to pay a player at the end of their contracts despite still owning their permits to play. The concept of the *passe* became so ingrained in Brazilian football's mentality that even now, decades after its extinction, people still use this outdated terminology. Most sporting media use expressions such as "a club bought a player's *passe*" when referring to player transfers between clubs. At the end of the day, the *passe* was an instrument of club control, discipline and power over the players; a condition that has been compared by many to a form of slavery.

So, what happened to Afonsinho? Why is he considered a ground-breaking figure in the South American football realm? Initially, it is important to understand that Afonsinho was a young, talented player during the late 1960s and early 1970s, a period known as the *"Anos de Chumbo"* ("Years of Lead") in Brazil's history. A military dictatorship ruled the country with an iron fist during those years. At the same time as the 1970 *Seleção* were enchanting Mexican audiences and the world with their impressive *jogo bonito* and the refined football skills of Pelé, Gérson, Rivelino, Tostão and co., a person could disappear from the streets of Rio de Janeiro or São Paulo, be incarcerated with no due process, and suffer barbaric torture. Political opposition was silenced, and guerrilla groups were decimated in the country's rural areas.

This was the political context when Afonsinho decided to challenge the *lei do passe* in the courts. If we look through a modern football lens and consider the billionaire figures in today's football, Afonsinho's reasons for starting legal action against his club might be seen as naïve. However, in a context where few players would contest anything that their clubs' managers said; and where defying sporting rules meant daring the dictatorship itself, Afonsinho was clearly a revolutionary. He is still perceived as a hero within Brazilian football circles today.

The Brazilian Bosman

Afonso Celso Garcia Reis, or Afonsinho, was not an ordinary player. While most professional players came from humble origins and had to leave school in their early years to pursue their sporting careers, Afonsinho had a degree as a physician. Furthermore, unlike most players who had no interest whatsoever in politics— nor in the country's social context, Afonsinho declared himself to be a communist.

Afonsinho was also a brilliant midfielder with an extraordinary tactical awareness that led him to deliver surprising assists to place strikers in perfect positions to score. Due to his skills, he became a leader on the field from a very young age, and little by little, he transferred that leadership to off-field situations where players were being exploited. Afonsinho could have chosen to stay quiet as he was part of a small group of elite professional players who received decent wages—while others could barely survive with their earnings as full-time footballers. Instead, his initial acts of rebellion were to fight his club because of low and belated wages, as well as unpaid prize money.

At 21 years old, Afonsinho was already an idol in Botafogo FC, a major Brazilian club in Rio de Janeiro, where Garrincha played nearly his whole life. The club's coach was Zagallo (who later replaced João Saldanha as the 1970 Seleção's coach) and Xisto Toniato was the club's vice-president designated to look after professional football. Toniato initially supported Afonsinho as the team's captain. However, as the player continued complaining about wage issues and how the club was treating the players, both Toniato and Zagallo soon blacklisted Afonsinho and dropped him from the team's starting line-up. They started to call him a negative leader. After a while, he was not even sitting on the bench. Afonsinho was totally ostracized. To the huge surprise of his teammates, he approached Zagallo for an explanation. Reports indicate that tough dialogue ensued, but no agreement was reached. Zagallo even criticized Afonsinho's long hair and beard, saying his appearance didn't suit a professional footballer.

Botafogo then decided to loan Afonsinho to Olaria, a small suburban club in Rio de Janeiro. In his early 20s and at the peak of his career, Afonsinho thought long and hard about a premature retirement from professional football. After a while though, he accepted the move, as he had to pay his mortgage among other financial commitments. However, his time in Olaria was only short, and after six months he was back to Botafogo. The length of his hair and beard had not changed, and the same issues with his appearance were brought up again by both Zagallo and Toniato. Toniato claimed that Afonsinho looked more like a rockstar than a football player. Playing the club's 'moral values' card, he decided that Afonsinho would not play for Botafogo until he shaved, and he was forbidden from even setting foot on the club's training fields.

The case for the 'free permit'

Humiliated and exhausted by the situation, Afonsinho contacted a lawyer to sue Botafogo. His lawyer claimed that Afonsinho was being restricted in his rights to practice his profession and wanted the link between the player and the club to end. Their complaint was heard in the State Sports Court, but they lost their case by just one vote (4–3). They then appealed to the Superior Court of Sport Justice, a Federal tribunal where Botafogo did not have the same power as they did in the State courts. After nine months, Afonsinho won his case: he became the first football player in Brazil to have a *passe livre*—a free license to play football.

Even the right-wing Jairzinho (the man who was the 1970 Seleção's top scorer) never won a *passe livre*. A player who scored twice in the Seleção's first game in Mexico against Czechoslovakia, and who scored a goal in each of the tournament's subsequent matches—a feat yet to be repeated by any other player in the world—was also humiliated by Botafogo. After Afonsinho, Jairzinho also went to the courts demanding his free license to play, but he lost his case. He was dropped from the team for three months, and only allowed to play again after publicly apologizing to the club.

Afonsinho never sold his *passe* to another club. He did not want to become enslaved by any other football manager. Instead, he leased his *passe* to the other clubs he played for during his career, such as Olaria, Santos, Vasco and Flamengo.

Afonsinho became a symbol of freedom in an era where players had to submit to their clubs' administrative rules if they wanted to practice their profession. He became a reference for many players and football supporters who wanted to learn more about his ordeal. His rebellion challenged not only the *lei do passe*, but also the whole oppressive system that submitted players within Brazilian football to the will of their club's management.

Moreover, in an authoritarian political context, Afonsinho's actions were also recognized as being resistance against broader tyranny. He gave interviews to alternative media outlets to contest the dictatorship and its censorship rules. These interviews appeared throughout the country. He talked about freedom and resistance, and he began to receive invitations to meet artists and musicians who were also trying to resist the authoritarian government through their work and songs.

Afonsinho was aware that his legal action against Botafogo cost him a potential spot in Brazil's national team. The national football confederation was dominated by people aligned with the army, and Afonsinho's enemies, such as coach Zagallo, controlled the team. So, despite his football skills, Afonsinho never had the chance to wear the Seleção's jersey. Nevertheless, he opened an avenue for the *lei do passe* to be questioned and finally abolished in 1998 with the enactment of the *Lei Pelé* (*Pelé* Law).

A free man

Afonsinho was acknowledged by Gilberto Gil, one of the greatest Brazilian poets, musicians and singers, who wrote a song in his honour in 1973. Titled *Meio de Campo* (Midfield), the beautiful song's lyrics include the following lines:

> *Dear friend Afonsinho*
> *I'm still right here*
> *Perfecting the imperfect*
> *Taking a break, finding a way*
> *Despising perfection*
> *As perfection is a goal*
> *Defended by the goalkeeper*
> *Who plays for the national team*
> *And I'm not Pelé*
> *But I can try to be Tostão'.*

In 1974, movie-maker Oswaldo Caldeira launched a documentary called Passe Livre where he not only tells Afonsinho's story but uses his saga to further criticize the military dictatorship. The movie won national awards and was considered a true portrayal of the oppression that footballers and Brazilian society in general were under during the "Years of Lead". In 2016, another movie called Barba, Cabelo & Bigode (Beard, Hair and Moustache) was launched by Lucio Branco to tell the story of Afonsinho and other players such as Paulo Cézar Lima (Caju) and Nei Conceição, who did not give up their freedom even when the army took control of football fields.

Afonsinho retired from football in 1981 at the age of 34. He practiced medicine for the next 30 years until his retirement when he moved to a small and quiet island next to Rio de Janeiro. In a 2018 interview, still with his beard—which was then white and well-trimmed—he expressed his nonconformity with the conservative political wave that was sweeping the world and reaching Brazil. He was outraged by the support of many Brazilian players for the then far-right candidate to the Presidency, Jair Bolsonaro. At 71, he was still talking to progressive and like-minded people, and drawing up plans to somehow change the orthodox mentality of Brazilian football.

More often than not, freedom fighters may not see the outcomes of their struggles during their lifetime. However, in a unique case within the South American football realm, Afonsinho was able to not only to achieve success for himself but also to pave the road for the freedom of many others after him.

Afonsinho's fight and victory were so grandiose that he was even recognized by football royalty. In a 1972 interview, King Pelé himself declared that he only knew one free man in football, and that was Afonsinho.

CHAPTER 9
A Black Panther on the field? Reinaldo, the goal-scorer who challenged a dictatorship

The year is 1978. Argentina is hosting the 11th FIFA World Cup. With a background of media censorship, political opponents' disappearance, torturing and killing, the football world moves towards the Southern Cone of South America to cheer on the best players in the world. The military despots who violently seized power in the country two years earlier intend to use the football tournament to sportswash their crimes. They have also made it clear to all delegations that they will not accept any demonstration that shows even minimal discontent with the country's political situation.

A little further north, Brazil prepares its team to bring home their fourth World Cup trophy. Leading their attack is Atlético Mineiro's Reinaldo, a 21-year-old striker who could not stop scoring goals in their national tournament. The team's coach is Cláudio Coutinho, a captain of the national army who was also the 1970 Seleção's fitness trainer. Before leaving for Argentina, the team joins an official farewell ceremony offered by dictator Ernesto Geisel, an army general who is occupying the Presidential chair of the country. In his speech to the team, Geisel echoes his Argentinian peers, and makes clear that he does not want to see any political manifestation on the fields: "Put personal feelings aside and make the team a closed group that can really bring victory." As if this message was not explicit enough, at the end of the ceremony Geisel comes closer to Reinaldo and delivers even stronger advice: "Go there and just play ball, my son. Leave the politics with us."

Later, already on Argentinian soil, André Richer, the head of the Brazilian team, has a further conversation with Reinaldo and reinforces the dictator's thoughts: both the military regime and the Brazilian Sports Confederation consider that the way he celebrates his goals is "too revolutionary". Further, Richer states that the Argentinian government would feel affronted and challenged by his goal celebration style. They strongly recommend that he does not repeat his celebratory gesture on the World Cup's pitches.

The fist up in the air

Then, the day arrives. Brazil play Sweden in both teams' debut in the 1978 World Cup. The Swedish team now holds the record of being the opponent that Brazil has played the most in World Cups: the Seleção has faced the Scandinavian side seven times in the world tournament, winning five matches and drawing twice. The 1978 match in early June would be their fourth World Cup encounter.

After a few goal chances for each side, Sjoberg, Sweden's number 10, opens the score early in the first half. Subsequently, his team tries to hold the fort against a Brazilian side that creates several goal chances but is unable to score any; the first half is coming to an end and the Seleção display a few signs of frustration. Then, in the last minute of the half, Toninho Cerezo crosses the ball behind the Swedish defence and into the penalty box. Reinaldo runs in followed by the European's last defender; with one touch the Brazilian number 9 controls the ball, beats his opponent and, as the goalkeeper jumps at his feet to try to take the ball from him, Reinaldo puts the ball over him with a second touch into the net.

Nobody knows what went through Reinaldo's mind after scoring that equalizer. The fact is, he did not have much time to reflect. Maybe in those milliseconds, his libertarian heart weighed all the political pressure he had received from the military, the Federation and even Brazil's President to curtail his customary but "too revolutionary" goal celebration.

Reinaldo then makes his decision: he stops running after three steps, still inside the goalkeeper's box, stands still, and with one foot parallel to the other, he releases

65

a big smile and raises his clenched right fist. He obviously saw no reason not to imitate the famous Black Panther's gesture which had gained worldwide attention when performed by African-American runners Tommie Smith and John Carlos during the 200-meter medal-presentation ceremony at the 1968 Olympic Games.

The mysterious memo

Reinaldo's gesture takes no more than two seconds before he raises his other arm as well and is quickly surrounded by his teammates who want to hug him and celebrate his goal together. However, its consequences lasted much longer than just that moment. A few days after the match, an anonymous letter arrives in the hotel hosting the Seleção during the World Cup. Coming from Venezuela and addressed to Reinaldo with no sender, the letter contains details of the infamous Operation Condor, a formal system of political repression established in 1975 that lasted until the early 1980s. Reuniting six countries in South America (Argentina, Brazil, Bolivia, Chile, Paraguay, and Uruguay) this murderous operation put a multinational collaboration in place that was aimed at eliminating political dissidents throughout the Southern Cone of South America.

In a 2009 interview, Reinaldo revealed how scared he was after reading that anonymous letter. He thought Operation Condor could be targeting him too. The letter also contained details about the death of Juscelino Kubitschek, the former Brazilian President who died in a car accident that many suspect was staged by the dictatorship to kill him. But Reinaldo didn't tell anyone on the team about the letter's contents during the World Cup—he simply tossed the document in his bags and did not touch it again until the event was over.

A socialist goal scorer

The second match for the Brazil squad in that World Cup was against Spain. The Brazilian team was quite lethargic during that match, and it ended goalless. Reinaldo was replaced during the second half by Roberto Dinamite and remained benched for the rest of the competition, coming back to the team only in the 2nd half of the 3rd place playoff against Italy that Brazil won 2-1 after goals were scored by Nelinho and Dirceu. As we know, Argentina won the World Cup for the first time in 1978, a triumph that remains tainted today by the qualms surrounding the Argentinian side's victory against Peru (6–0), but mainly by the enormous amount of pressure that the Argentine dictators put on the team to succeed to make their sportswashing efforts worthwhile.

Reinaldo still claims that he was sacked from the team due to his political resistance. However, the fact is that Reinaldo had physical issues. During the competition he was training with long pants so the press would not see his swelled knees.

José Reinaldo de Lima, known as 'Reinaldo', or just 'Rei' (the Portuguese word for 'King') became a professional footballer in 1973 when he was only 16. His professional career lasted 15 years, and during most of that time (12 years) he played for Atlético Mineiro, a major football club from the south-eastern State of Minas Gerais. Nowadays, Reinaldo continues to hold the honourable title of the greatest idol of the *Galo* (Portuguese for 'rooster', the club's nickname), and its passionate fans often pay tribute to him during important matches at their home stadium.

In the 1977 Brazilian Championship, Reinaldo played 18 matches for Atlético, scoring 28 goals. This feat means that he still holds the highest goal average per game record in the history of the Brazilian Championship: 1.55 goals per match. In 1978, during Atlético's 6–0 victory against América—RN, he scored what is deemed to be the most beautiful goal ever scored in the *Mineirão* Stadium. To celebrate his prowess, the local Federation built a plaque that is still visible at the stadium's entrance even after its renovations for the 2014 World Cup.

Goals followed Reinaldo everywhere he played, making him widely acclaimed around the country. Unfortunately, his knee issues also plagued him. Having started as a professional in his adolescence, he tore his menisci in 1974 when he tripped in a hole on a field. This injury was aggravated by a tackle in a training session, and in 1976 he underwent surgery to have both menisci removed. This procedure was later thought to be unnecessary by several specialists. However, he kept playing to a high level until he was 31 when the pain caused by his knee troubles forced him into an early retirement.

In the months leading up to the 1978 World Cup, and after his brilliant performances in his Atlético Mineiro's jersey where he was scoring goal after goal, the Brazilian sporting media insisted that he should be the owner of the number 9 jersey. Journalists were saying that regardless of the tactics the coach wanted to implement with the team, Reinaldo needed to be the team's striker. However, a few months before the mega sports event, Reinaldo gave an interview to *Movimento*, a leftist newspaper. Founded in 1975 during the dictatorship but at a time when the political system was suffering its initial cracks that would later lead to its termination, *Movimento* had several contributors who were still living abroad in political exile.

A few considered that Reinaldo was naïve in exposing his political ideals as he did in that interview. After all, the oppressive regime was still in charge, and the World Cup was just a few months away. Nevertheless, Reinaldo opened his mind to *Movimento*, and positioned himself in favour of all resurgent unionist movements in the country; he particularly called for a players' union to fight for players' rights. Further, Reinaldo defended the claims for a political amnesty to allow exiled Brazilians to come back to the country and defended the notion that the nation needed a new constitution.

Clearly, that interview would not have sounded good to the military. Would Heleno Nunes, the admiral who was also the president of the CBD, tolerate such 'socialist' ideas? What early on was a national, unanimous view for Reinaldo to play a key role in the team became more doubtful.

However, Reinaldo's popularity was such that neither the Federation nor the coach had the 'balls' to sideline him before the event. He went to the World Cup, but at the first opportunity, he was benched.

After all these years, Reinaldo is still sought by the national and international press to discuss both football and political topics. In a 2018 interview with the Brazilian edition of the global newspaper *El País*, he pondered that in 1978 he was benched due to a direct order from Admiral Heleno Nunes. Additionally, in the same interview he stated that after the World Cup, "hidden forces of the fascist regime" started to disseminate rumours about his personal life. Gossip about his sexual orientation started to appear in popular radio programs; a defamatory campaign spreading that he was a drunk, a drug-addict and a homosexual was also circulated in the mainstream media. "It was a moral lynching, and I had nobody to support me, no political party, no union, I was just by myself," he said.

In 1982, Reinaldo was not called up to the Seleção for their World Cup campaign in Spain. Telê Santana, who was a football genius, was also an apologist for traditional moral values. He overtly declared that he did not want a homosexual in his team—but in the end, he said that Reinaldo's physical troubles caused him to be eliminated from the team's list.

Reinaldo disputes Telê's version of events. He argues that he was fit and in good health at the time, and that there was political influence over the coaching team to leave him out of the Seleção's line-up. He considers that many powerful people still could not swallow his lifestyle nor his socialist ideas.

No regrets

After his retirement, Reinaldo battled against drug addiction and tried to enter politics; he also worked as a football coach, and nowadays is still connected to his former club, working as a scout for Atlético's youth squads. He has never regretted doing the Black Panther sign at the World Cup in Argentina. He is proud of all his political struggles within the football world. Considering football as a *machista* and orthodox environment, Reinaldo believes that as a public figure he needed to step up against the autocratic regime. At the end of the day, he believes that his actions, as symbolic as they were, accelerated the democratic process in Brazil.

One thing is certain: not many footballers would have had the courage to raise their fists like a Black Panther in front of feared, cold, bloodthirsty and murderous South American dictators.

Reinaldo had it.

CHAPTER 10
Sócrates: Elegance and political fight—on and off the pitches

Tall. Elegant. Smoker. *Futebol-arte* icon. Medical doctor. Master of the 'back heel'. Political activist. Captain of the national team. The list goes on.

Among so many world-class footballers who have worn the Seleção's jersey in the past 90 years, nobody equals Sócrates. Part of the magic squad who enchanted the football world at the 1982 World Cup in Spain, he scored the first Brazilian goal in the match against Italy that became known as the '*Sarrià Tragedy*'. He also missed a penalty in the penalty shootout against France at the 1986 World Cup in Mexico.

Nevertheless, Sócrates had many other facets that made him both a distinctive footballer among his peers and an unforgettable man. He was a politically aware citizen who used his high-profile position as a player at one of the most popular Brazilian football clubs (S.C. Corinthians) to struggle for democracy and civil liberties both inside and outside the sporting milieu.

I am glad to have spent my teen years in São Paulo city where I could not only watch Sócrates displaying his unique style on the football fields—many times against my beloved São Paulo FC—but where I have also been able to participate in a few key political moments in Brazil's journey towards democracy. One of those historical passages happened in April 1984 during a warm autumn São Paulo evening.

My beloved mum and I were among nearly two million citizens who protested in a massive public park known as '*Vale do Anhangabaú*' in the core of Brazil's most populated city. It was the principal rally of a social crusade that had started seven months earlier and gained traction across the streets of all medium-sized cities as well as all the capital cities of all states in Brazil. In all these demonstrations, nonviolent activists sported white ribbons on their heads and displayed posters and standards proclaiming, "Free Elections Now!" It was the *diretas-já* movement where Brazilians demanded to elect their own President, a civil right that was taken from them 20 years earlier by the 1964 military coup d'état.

This demonstration in the *Vale do Anhangabaú* was a critical one as it was taking place just one week prior to the National Congress assembly that would vote on the bill that could restore free elections in the country. On the edge of the *Vale do Anhangabaú* was a giant stage full of musicians, intellectuals, entertainers, and politicians waiting for their time to sing, chant or speak. The sanctioned speakers of the night were well-known left-wing leaders. Many of them had been exiled abroad during the military dictatorship, but they were back in Brazil due to the 1979 Amnesty Law. In addition to traditional politicians, emerging leaders such as Lula, the unionist who later became the most popular President of the country, were also programmed to speak.

Among these sanctioned speakers on the stage was the tall and thin figure of Sócrates (also known as '*Magrão*' to his close friends —meaning 'big, skinny person'). Despite the anxious and noisy atmosphere of this important civic demonstration, when it was Sócrates' turn to speak, the mob went silent. His speech was simple, straightforward, and showed his commitment to the country's democracy. Sócrates was at the peak of his footballing days and had already received several lucrative proposals to play for European sides. However, at that moment, he vowed in front of millions of his compatriots that if the bill was approved in the Parliament, he would not accept any well-paid offer from overseas clubs. He swore that he would be glad to play in a "new and democratic country". He also said that if the bill was defeated, he would make his way to Italy as it would be inconceivable for him to stay in an undemocratic society.

Sócrates was one of the most cheered speakers of the night. Unfortunately, to his frustration—and to the disappointment of my parents and hundreds of millions of Brazilians—a week later the bill was defeated. He left the country to play for Fiorentina in Italy where he lasted just one season before returning to Brazil.

Sócrates' playing style and his political activism had a solid influence not only in the football world but also on the Brazilian social order. The combination of his sporting career and his political activity is one of the most cited examples around the world of political renovation through sport, or what progressive academics and activists call "sport for social change". The rest of this chapter outlines the facets of Sócrates' fascinating and complex life. I hope this will make it clear that he surpassed the football pitch to become much more than a sports myth—he is a libertarian icon who can encourage every freedom fighter around the world.

Sócrates and football-art

Sócrates once stated that football seemed to be a "route accident" in his life. He thought he was not destined to be a decent player. However, a closer look over his life helps us to better appreciate how his football elegance advanced. Sócrates didn't *just* play football: he played *futebol-arte* (football-art, or *jogo bonito*) which is more than just a game style; it is inextricably linked to autonomy. *Futebol-arte* is liberty.

Sócrates Brasileiro Sampaio de Souza Vieira de Oliveira was born in 1954 in *Belém do Pará*, the capital city of *Pará*, a State situated in the North Region of Brazil near the Amazon Forest. He was six when his family moved to Ribeirão Preto, a medium-sized city in the State of São Paulo. Like many Brazilian players, he started playing futsal at school, and at the age of 14, he and other school colleagues were called by Haroldo Soares, their school coach, to play for Botafogo de Ribeirão Preto, one of the two major teams in the city. It was in this team that Sócrates began to shape his reputation as an artistic player. When he finished high school, he enrolled in university, which is a rare pathway for Brazilian professional footballers. Yet, trying to reconcile football practices, weekend tournaments and lessons at medical school was very tough. He was only able to achieve it because of the support he received from his coaches and managers at Botafogo-RP. Acknowledging his outstanding talent, they allowed him to attend his medical classes and just show up for the weekend matches. He usually played in them after doing 24-hour hospital shifts.

This lack of training did not help him to develop the necessary muscular strength to cope with the harsh conditions on the football field where opponents would chase and tackle skilled forwards. Seeing himself as an 'anti-athlete', Sócrates quickly adopted an alternative playing method that was entirely opposed to what was played on the pitches in those times; he started to use just one touch to pass the ball. That was his strategy to avoid body contact with his adversaries. He used any part of his body to make the ball run, but particularly his heels with surprising and magic touches that later became his trademark.

Another possible explanation for Sócrates' playing style might be the discrepancy between his stature and his small feet—as this disparity was so large, he would go down or become unstable if he twisted his body too quickly. Hence, he learned the back-heel kick to overcome his 'natural problem'.

However, many commentators maintain that Sócrates' astonishing back-heel passes had just one purpose: to not just gain the attention of fans, but their emotions. For those analysts, his back-heel touches were a deep celebration of *futebol-arte*.

For ten years (2001 to 2011), Sócrates also wrote chronicles to *Carta Capital*, a left-oriented Brazilian weekly magazine. In one of these pieces, he confessed in a cheerful and almost childlike way how he used the back-heel trick to attract the fans' admiration. When telling the story of a commemorative match to celebrate a famous Brazilian singer, he says that, in a stadium packed with 30,000 fans:

> I played the whole game using back hell kicks; the crowd went crazy in each touch; it was a collective catharsis; it was so good to look to the stands and see that happiness (...). At the end of the game, I kicked a penalty with my heel. The ball touched the bar. Never a missed penalty was so cheered!

Has Sócrates incorporated Garrincha's *futebol-arte* spirit and style? They surely were two of the finest examples of artists on the football field; they both learned to overcome physical issues—Garrincha with his bent legs, and Sócrates with his small feet—to enhance their playing potential and transform their ball touches with artistic excellence. They both might have been inspired by one of the greatest South American writers, the Argentinian Jorge Luis Borges, who once wrote:

A writer, or any man, must believe that whatever happens to him is an instrument; everything has been given for an end. This is even stronger in the case of the artist (...) all has been given like clay, like material for one's art. One must accept it. (Seven Nights, p.385).

Sócrates' professional career

As recently as October 2022, the influential UK football magazine *FourFourTwo* released a new ranking of the 100 best football players of all time. Despite the controversies that always surround these types of lists, you only need to look at his ranking to understand the relevance of Sócrates in the world football context. According to *FourFourTwo*, he is the 29th-best player of all time, above *Ballon d'Or* winners such as Italian Roberto Baggio (40th) or World Cup champions like Argentinian Daniel Passarella (58th). According to *FourFourTwo*, "this intellectual footballer defined an entire generation in Brazil with his performances in [the] 1982 and 1986 World Cups".

Sócrates began to attract contract proposals from major Brazilian teams in the late 1970s when he was playing in magic fashion for *Botafogo de Ribeirão Preto*, then a regional, medium-sized club in São Paulo. Nevertheless, as he was adamant he would complete his medical degree, he decided not to sign for any other club until graduating from his university studies. When he did, he turned his total focus to football.

In 1978, he accepted an offer from Vicente Matheus, the legendary and autocratic president of the powerhouse Sport Club Corinthians, one of the most popular football clubs in Brazil. It was the start of a relationship that would quickly transform not only Sócrates and Corinthians' lives, but also leave an undeniable imprint on Brazil's football and social history.

In those times, S.C. Corinthians was the club that best embodied the underprivileged internal migrants from the Brazilian north and north-east who escaped massive droughts, starvation, and poverty to take their chance in the big metropolis. A large portion of this population was also socially ostracized for being black or *mulatos* residents of the city's slums. They had a strong, intense, and fanatic connection with the club, and called themselves "The Faithful". They did not expect any massive, beautiful performance nor *futebol-arte* from the players; however, they demanded an almost religious commitment to the team. They wanted the Corinthians' players to learn that they were in a war, and to win it; players must leave everything they had on the field—their sweat, flesh, and blood.

It was not a surprise that their world views clashed with Sócrates' playful elegance. While he used to deliver quick passes when he had ball possession, as he did not have much speed, he inflicted a slower pace in the game—this was a different tempo that The Faithful was not used to. It took more than two years and a few State titles for them to build a positive relationship with him. At the beginning, the *Corinthianos* (Corinthians fans) resented his apparent lack of passion: in an interview Sócrates declared that he wanted "to be a professional, not a warrior"—exactly the opposite of what fans were expecting from their major and expensive signing.

Fans were used to players who demonstrated their virility and gave their blood and heart to the team. It was hard for them to swallow Sócrates' refinement, art, and intelligence. They mostly resented his alleged lack of passion. Sócrates confirmed that some journalists produced the fable that all Corinthians players had to be ignorant and animated troopers; as he was quite the reverse, the fans opposed him—and even tried to lynch him once after a defeat in the National Championship.

Nevertheless, after a few brilliant on-field displays, goals, and trophies, Sócrates managed to improve his standing with The Faithful. Moreover, he was able to transform the way they cheered for the team; instead of the team rushing in the same quick pace as the crowd's chants and drums, led by the wand of 'maestro' Sócrates, the mob began to change their tempo.

Sócrates also had struggles with the president of the club, the legendary Vicente Matheus. He had contract battles with the club and even stopped playing for two months in 1980 after failing to reach an agreement. He claimed that the dispute was not just over money but also rights and principles. After this dispute, and after Matheus offered him better conditions, he was convinced by friends—including the acclaimed football journalist Juca Kfouri and fans—to sign the contract and return to the club.

However, his reappearance marked a new period in his relationship with the Corinthians. After being away for nearly two months, Sócrates presented himself with a beard and long hair. It looked like he was not only transforming the way The Faithful supported the team; he was also being changed *by* them. He was determined to mix his intellectual *futebol-arte* with the more instinctive style demanded by the team's fans. It was the start of a new and stronger emotional bond between the fans and their idol. It worked very well for both sides. Sócrates played almost five years for Corinthians, appearing in 297 games where he scored 172 goals. He gained three State Championships and is classified as one of the top 10 players in the club's history.

After leaving the club in 1984, Sócrates played for Fiorentina (Italy), and two other great Brazilian teams, Flamengo and Santos, before hanging up his boots. Nevertheless, for him nothing was the same as playing in Corinthians. He uttered these feelings by saying that to play for Corinthians one had to show uncontested love. For him, Corinthians was more than a club—it was a nation made up of a distinctive culture and unique people. He wrote that to play for the club was "like being called up to an irrational war and never questioning that it is the most important war that ever existed. It is being requested to think as Marx, fight as Napoleon, pray as Dalai-Lama and donate your life just like Mandela."

Sócrates also played for the Seleção. He was always aware of the institutional weight that the national team and its 'magic' yellow jersey have for the Brazilian identity.

Despite being short-listed for the team who would play the 1978 World Cup in Argentina, he did not make the final cut—probably because he was still playing for Botafogo and not for a powerhouse like Corinthians. After 1978, though, he was a recurring name in the team, and was the captain of the *Sele*ção when they lost against Italy in the *Sarrià Tragedy* in the 1982 Spain World Cup.

Sócrates treasured the 1982 team. He was elated by playing in that World Cup. He considers that team to be the best he ever played for in his career. Being its captain was "the major honour I ever had in my life," he said. The 1982 *Sele*ção had a playing style that he thought represented the players' feelings, their principles, and the way they lived and cried. He described his goal in his World Cup debut against the Soviet Union as an "endless orgasm". By contrast, he considers the *Sarrià Tragedy* as his life's saddest moment and most important lesson. After the catastrophic downfall, as he had no other aims in his life than winning the World Cup, he had to "start again from zero".

His rapport with Telê Santana, the master of *futebol-arte*, was vital to Sócrates' time in the *Seleção*. He felt at home in the team, they had a close connection, and they chatted about everything—Sócrates relished being able to debate game plans with coaches and other players. Most of all, both had *futebol-arte* rooted in their souls.

Sócrates and Telê made another appearance on the world stage at the 1986 Mexico World Cup. His memories from this tournament though are different and painful. According to Sócrates, the 1986 team had a 1982 soul, but was plagued by key players' unhealed injuries. His missed penalty against France cost Brazil's qualification in the quarter-finals of the championship, and Sócrates did not sleep that night.

He made 60 appearances in the yellow jersey, scoring 22 goals. Even if he did not win a title with the *Seleção*, he wrote one of the most beautiful chapters in the team's history. Furthermore, Sócrates used his position as a Corinthians and Seleção football star to build a platform for social change by struggling against any type of injustice.

Sócrates and democracy

Sócrates believed that sport was a commanding and cost-effective way to promote education and progress; he promoted this idea every chance he had. That's why he used his role as a leader in the Corinthians team to create and advance a movement called 'Corinthians Democracy'.

Established in 1981 by a cluster of professional footballers who wanted to have a say in their own working lives, Corinthians Democracy promptly gained exposure in the pages of the main Brazilian newspapers. Most importantly, the movement happened in a popular football club in a period where Brazilians were fighting to recover their democratic rights that had been suppressed by the military dictatorship since 1964. The 1979 Amnesty Law brought back many politicians, artists and scholars who had been expatriated from the country. Furthermore, numerous demonstrations and strikes were happening across the country; workers, students and women were marching and demanding civil rights and better life conditions.

These circumstances made the Corinthians Democracy a huge vehicle that brought issues of basic civil rights into the homes of millions of Brazilians who did not have access to other information sources. Taking advantage of monocratic president Vicente Matheus leaving the club, leading players such as Sócrates, Wladimir and Casagrande demanded that their voice be heard in every decision about their professional lives. Their initial plea was the abolition of the 'confinement' practice before matches where players needed to stay in a hotel overnight prior to any match, regardless of whether it was a home game or not.

From then onwards, players started to vote for everything that concerned their collective working life: from the practice timetable to the days or times they would travel to a match in another city, and even the hotel where they would stay. The playing group became used to the democratic process. Other professionals involved in the team's everyday operations—doctors, coaches, directors and even the most modest staff (such as cleaners, bus drivers, and cooks) were each entitled to one vote. The Corinthians Democracy could be defined as a movement with a philosophical background based on the universal suffrage's motto: "One person, one vote".

It is important to bear in mind that everything that happens with Corinthians has huge repercussions within society: losing or winning, the Corinthians make Brazilian newspapers' front pages every day. The Corinthians Democracy quickly made its way to media headlines, bringing all its controversies to public debate. It also became a central source for the civil rights movement, and its leaders took advantage of their visibility to bring relevant democratic messages to the wider public.

In December 1983, 115,000 fans went to the Morumbi Stadium to watch the State Championship Final. Corinthians was playing my beloved São Paulo FC. I was there in the São Paulo crowd, cheering on my team. Nevertheless, I must confess that I admired what the Corinthians players did that night.

Just prior to the initial whistle when both teams made their entrance onto the pitch, the whole Corinthians side marched around the field with a massive banner upon which was written: "Winning or losing, but always with democracy". In the centre of their procession, holding the banner, we could see the tallest man on the field—Sócrates, with his white head ribbon, naturally leading the demonstration.

You could not imagine a clearer connection between the "Free Elections Now!" movement and the Corinthians Democracy.

At the beginning of 1984, the Corinthians Democracy was prominent and the "Free Elections Now!" was at its pinnacle. Sócrates was actively involved with different forms of democratic action, such as fundraising matches for civil rights issues, or the foundation of the workers' party (PT). In these instances, he would leave the football context and meet with artists, politicians, and other intellectuals. He later described these occasions as "orgasmic moments of Brazilian-ness".

Sócrates' legacy

In many Carnaval parades, while regular people are dancing in the streets, famous football players are partying heavily within VIP areas. They briefly leave their drinks inside and come to the windows to say hello to their fans, trying to show a wholesome image to the public.

Sócrates considered these to be hypocritical performances. He thought that we should agree that all players drink, and that he himself enjoyed a few beers. He once declared that—against the will of the powers that be—he was a drinker, a smoker, and a thinker.

In my early teens, my friends and I used to go to the Pacaembu Stadium in the heart of São Paulo city to watch the Sunday afternoon matches. If we were lucky enough, my friend's uncle would oversee a turnstile and let us crawl underneath it! After the games, we walked to a traditional cafeteria in the neighbourhood to have some burgers and a chocolate milkshake. There, in a humble table on an isolated corner, we frequently saw Sócrates reading the newspaper, enjoying his beer and his cigarette, totally alone. No fans, no security guards, no helpers. It was the man by himself, crafting his next football and political move.

I wish I had the courage on those days to interrupt the big man's meditation to have a conversation with him. Maybe I would ask him if his right fist, gripped in the air to celebrate his goals, was a way to mimic the Black Panthers' gesture. I can just imagine his response: he would ask me to notice that, together with his rebellious attitude, there was always a smile. You must struggle without missing the joyfulness of play and life.

Sócrates passed away in 2011, leaving an inspiring heritage of joy, *futebol-arte* and freedom struggles. In 2022, during the acclaimed *Ballon d'Or* awards ceremony held by the prestigious *France Football Magazine*, a new prize named after Sócrates was presented to Senegalese international Sadio Mané. The *Sócrates Award* will be granted every year in recognition of footballers whose efforts go far beyond the pitch—those who carry out exceptional humanitarian and social work.

The *Sócrates Award* is an incredible global and enduring recognition of Sócrates' libertarian legacy. Sócrates must certainly be smiling now, as his ideas and struggles have prevailed over the ideologies and practices of the corrupt and authoritarian elite who he fought against during his time with us.

CHAPTER 11

No Mercy for Despots: The *hinchadas* with memory

José Nino Gavazzo was a Uruguayan army colonel who was the chief of his country's branch of the notorious Operation Condor. This operation was an international collaboration between several South American countries. It functioned across borders between the mid-1970s to the early 1980s, aiming to systematically exterminate political opponents. Gavazzo held the 'record' of court convictions due to his crimes during the Uruguayan dictatorship: 28 homicides, including the kidnapping and disappearance of María Claudia García Irureta-Goyena, the daughter-in-law of Argentinian writer Juan Gelman, winner of the 2007 Miguel de Cervantes Prize. Gavazzo lived in home detention and passed away in June 2021 aged 81 without confessing to all his crimes, nor detailing where some of his victims' remains were hidden.

"Ni olvido ni perdón"—"neither forget nor forgive". This was the sentence written on the banner that the players of Villa Española, a humble club from Montevideo, the Uruguayan capital city, displayed on the field before their match against the powerful Peñarol just after Gavazzo's passing, and on the eve of the 48th anniversary of the military coup that established a dictatorship in their country. Villa Española's goalkeeper scored a last-minute goal from midfield to level the contest at 1-1. However, the images that went viral across the world were not those of this epic goal, but pictures of the players' demonstration, and images of Villa Española's greatest goal scorer, midfielder "Bigote" López. He sported a black T-shirt before and after the match that had this strong reference to Gavazzo emblazoned on it: "Te fuiste sin hablar, cobarde—

You left without speaking, coward."

This demonstration against Gavazzo—who according to Bigote was "neither more nor less the most detestable person in Uruguay"—was just a small portion of a broader movement of transitional justice that started in Argentina and spread to Uruguay and Chile. Transitional justice is a method to address organized or immense abuses of human rights that mutually offer reparation to victims of these violations and produces or increases prospects for the renovation of the political structures that might have been at the centre of the crimes against humanity. Transitional justice processes use four structural pillars to achieve their objectives: truth-seeking (usually via truth commissions and other historical research mechanisms), the prosecution of suspects of massive human rights violations, compensations to victims, and institutional reforms so that these crimes can never be repeated.

The movie 'Argentina, 1985', directed by Santiago Mitre and launched in 2022 is a portrait of how the country dealt with its transitional justice procedures. It's a painful and tense true story that shows the extensive crimes committed by Jorge Rafael Videla, the Argentinian dictator who was at the top of the military junta that commanded the country during the 1978 FIFA World Cup. The movie shows how Videla was finally condemned to perpetual prison. He passed away in prison in 2013 and was buried under a false name in a cemetery on the outskirts of Buenos Aires.

These movements that seek truth and reparations have disseminated across all societal sectors in Argentina, Uruguay, and Chile. Football, with its huge relevance throughout these societies, is a key component of the struggle for remembrance and historical reparations. Beyond players' demonstrations, these battles have been seen on the terraces where hinchas (football supporters) have started to identify human rights abusers among their members, and to call for justice within their football clubs.

Dictators expelled

In the early 1970s, Club Social y Deportivo Colo-Colo (or Colo-Colo) was the main Chilean football club. They were so significant within Chile's society that in 1971,

Salvador Allende (the socialist President who would later be ejected from power by Pinochet's coup-d'état) stated that only Colo-Colo could unite Chileans over any cause, even though he was a supporter of Colo-Colo's rival La U (Club Universidad de Chile). Once in power, brutal dictator Augusto Pinochet was quick to organise the club's management to nominate him as the honorary president of Colo-Colo.

Coerced by the dictator's brutal tyranny, Colo-Colo members waited for justice for many years. They had to wait until 2015 for an assembly of the club's members to approve the erasing of all records of the dictator from the club's history. In the minutes of that meeting, they noted that the appointment of Pinochet as member and honorary president of their club was "illegal and illegitimate".

This Colo-Colo supporters' action generated momentum among South American football clubs and their supporters to establish truth in their histories and reinstate justice among their memberships.

Following the Chilean example, on 24 March 2021 (the annual day when Argentinians celebrate their National Day of Remembrance for Truth and Justice), the powerhouse Boca Juniors held a ceremony to remember the 30,000 people who disappeared in the country during the period known as State Terrorism. Alongside members of the world-renowned human rights movement Mothers (and Grandmothers) of Plaza de Mayo, the president of the Argentinian Football Federation, the Boca Junior's president, and the captains of both Boca Juniors and Defensores de Belgrano planted a tree to honour all those who fought the dictatorship.

At the same time, the club announced the dissolution of the membership and the positions held at the club by agents and leaders of the dictatorship, such as Emilio Eduardo Massera. Admiral Massera, who was granted the title of honorary member of the club in 1972, was one of the three members of the military junta who led the dictatorship during 1976 and 1978, after the coup d'état that removed Isabelita Perón from the Presidency.

Hinchas con memoria (fans with memory)

Acclaimed Uruguayan journalist Eduardo Galeano, author of 'Soccer in Sun and Shadow', once wrote that "Uruguay does not have history, instead it has football".

To overcome this and reinstitute historical truth, during the late 2010s several Uruguayan football supporters' groups commenced new political campaigns to both remember the crimes their countries' dictatorships committed against members of their clubs, and to expel people from their associations who had been found guilty of severe abuses during the military reign.

In 2021, the hinchas con memoria (fans with memory) movement formed by supporters of the Uruguayan Club Atlético Peñarol celebrated the final achievements of their 2018 crusade called Gol contra la Impunidad (a Goal Against Impunity). This campaign expelled Gavazzo and Manuel Cordero from the club as both had been convicted for their participation and leadership during Operation Condor. During this celebration, young supporters were joined by Alba González, an 87-year-old mother whose son, Rafael Lezama, disappeared in 1976 during Operation Condor in Argentina. Despite her age, Alba González was still an active participant of Uruguayan associations of mothers and relatives of people who had disappeared during the military government. This was a symbolic moment that showed how different generations of Uruguayans are unified and strong in their fight for remembrance and justice.

It is important to remark that at the start of its activities in 2018, the Goal Against Impunity campaign had already achieved the ban of Miguel Zuluaga from Peñarol membership. Zuluaga was a brutal torturer who worked for Uruguay's intelligence department during the military dictatorship. His interrogation methods were so ruthless that his colleagues nicknamed him El Zulu. Despite his role in the disappearance and killing of countless Uruguayans, Zuluaga was employed by the Uruguayan Football Association and worked as head of security for the national team from 2000 to 2018, until he was finally fired after intense social pressure that started with the Peñarol hinchas campaign. Pictures of Zuluaga hugging Uruguayan striker and former Barcelona player Luis Suárez or shaking hands with celebrated Uruguayan national coach Óscar Tabárez could be seen in placards during the Peñarol supporters' street protests. Zuluaga's story is clear evidence of the complex and problematic relationship between football and politics in Uruguay.

During the same period, a group of supporters of the Club Nacional de Football (which, along with Peñarol are the two main football clubs in Uruguay), created an anti-fascist flank. The objective of this subgroup was to collect stories of fans about their experiences cheering on their club during the dictatorship. It offered a few online channels for fans to share their stories. The national hinchas committed to respecting the privacy and anonymity of anyone willing to share what happened in the club during those dark times. In the open letter they sent to all Nacional supporters, they said that they need to "Listen. Remember. Make visible. Not to forget, nor to repeat. To keep fighting."

Football and transitional justice

Reparation for victims is as important for transitional justice as the prosecution of culprits. It can involve money when victims seek compensation for financial difficulties they suffered after their family providers were killed by the barbaric political regimes that disgraced South America in the 1970s and 1980s. However, reparation also includes symbolic acts that will re-establish truth and preserve historical memories.

Bearing this in mind, in October 2021 Argentinian Club Atlético Huracán paid tribute to eight of its members who disappeared during the dictatorship. In a touching ceremony that took place at their home ground (Estadio Tomás A. Ducó in Buenos Aires), the club reissued the members' identifications and offered them to their families. The club also commissioned an artistic montage in honour of them. This artwork has human rights as its central theme, and it was installed on a wall in the club's stadium to preserve the memory of those who suffered atrocities during the military period.

Transitional justice is an ongoing process in many South American societies. While much has already been achieved, there is still more work to be done to recover the truth, prosecute and punish the culprits, and compensate victims and their families. There are countries such as Brazil, the largest South American nation, where the process has been slowed down by right-wing governments. Even though a few Brazilian families have received compensation, no criminal or torturer has been convicted.

Nevertheless, in Argentina, Chile and Uruguay, football has helped to achieve transitional justice objectives for institutions, victims, and culprits. In all these nations, being in a football grandstand is so relevant for community cohesion that the idea of cheering on your beloved club alongside someone who committed crimes against humanity was unbearable for them.

CHAPTER 12

The Yellow Shirt Controversy: Social class struggle and the future of South American civilization

On the brink of the 2014 Brazil World Cup, the mixed feelings of Brazilian people towards the tournament were clear: on the one hand, they were emphatic in demonstrating their love to their national team, the *Seleção;* on the other hand, Brazilians were angry with FIFA for the suspicions of corruption that surrounded the tournament.

These contradictory attitudes towards the national team were rooted in their undemocratic past where authoritarian governments used the Seleção's victories to reinforce their tyranny. In that period, guerrilla groups who fought the ruling military tried to show their political opposition by barracking *against* the Seleção—but without much success, as when the national team was playing a decisive World Cup match, guerrilla fighters could not help themselves. Almost without realizing it, they became supporters in front of their TV sets.

Since 2014, Brazilians have been living in political turmoil. Just after the World Cup, a Presidential election divided the country: then President Dilma Rousseff was re-elected by the narrowest margin in the country's history till that moment, beating her rival in the run-off voting by just 3%. This political divide reflected society: families were split due to their candidate choice, long-term friendships were disrupted, and anger overflowed from social media channels to the streets where heated arguments between different political partisans were common.

However, a few months after her re-election, Rousseff faced an unprecedented political campaign against her Presidency: parties that lost the election along with many in the urban middle-class were unhappy with the country's shaky economy. They started to protest. Initially, the protesters went to their apartment windows in the main Brazilian cities in the evening and hit their kitchen pans to make noise every time the President appeared on the TV news: the sound could be heard everywhere. After a while, they took to the streets to demonstrate their disapproval towards Rousseff's policies. Soon afterwards, the Parliamentary speaker accepted and lodged an impeachment request against the President.

Right-wing movements kept the momentum going with the help of major national TV broadcasters and State governments. Many more protesters hit the streets voicing their anger against the Federal government. In May 2016, Rousseff was temporarily removed from her position by the lower house. Just after the 2016 Rio Olympics, she was impeached and left her seat. The allegations against her were flawed, but most Senators voted for her impeachment anyway. Her deputy, Michel Temer, who was actively supporting the impeachment campaign, took over the Presidency. In her farewell speech, Rousseff predicted: "We will be back".

The yellow jersey as a far-right political symbol

Amid all this political turmoil, football, the Seleção, and in particular, the national team's jersey, played a major role.

The Seleção's yellow jersey was the chosen symbol of the movement demanding Rousseff's impeachment. Led by conservative parties and far-right political forces, the pro-impeachment protesters transformed the streets of the country's main cities in a yellow sea. To prove their alleged patriotism and loyalty to the country, millions of people used the Brazilian football team's jersey during their 2015–16 demonstrations against Rousseff.

In a society that was already split by the 2014 Presidential elections, the use of the Seleção's yellow jersey by conservative political powers proved to be socially divisive. The 'yellow vs red' war was the most powerful representation of the ongoing social class struggle in South America's largest country. On the one side there were the 'yellows', the middle- and upper-classes who detested Rousseff and the Workers' Party's (PT's) social policies, all dressed in the number one CBF shirt; on the other side, were the 'reds'. They were the PT supporters and other more left-leaning people who believed that Rousseff's impeachment had been a coup-d'état and claimed support for democracy and social justice.

This symbolic division did not stop in 2016. Even after the President's impeachment, the political turmoil persisted. 'Operation Car Wash' was a controversial but well-supported national investigation against corruption. It landed major businessmen and political leaders in jail, including the former Parliamentary speaker (the one who had allowed Rousseff's impeachment process to go through the legal channels) and Rio's Governor, among other high-profile politicians. Finally, in April 2018, Operation Car Wash jailed Luiz Inacio Lula da Silva, the former Brazilian President (2002–2010) and frontrunner in every poll for the 2018 Presidential election.

During all these moments, the yellow jersey campaigners were on the streets showing their 'commitment' to the nation, their opposition to the Workers' Party's social policies, and their alleged disgust towards unproven corrupt practices. They absolutely kidnapped the nation's symbols, such as the national flag and anthem and, of course, the once-loved Seleção yellow jersey.

However, the real intentions behind Rousseff's impeachment quickly became clear: new President Michel Temer started to cancel all social policies that characterised the Workers' Party's period in government, sending millions back to poverty and hunger that had almost disappeared over the past decade in the country. He also voted in favour of laws to abolish workers' rights that had been in place for the past 80 years, leading millions into insecure and precarious working conditions. The political turmoil did not ease, and the yellow jersey became a sign of conservative and 'anti-people' policies. The jersey that was once the symbol of a winning nation, and that all Brazilians used to wear when traveling overseas to show their 'Brazilian-ness', had been undeniably captured by a political group. The ones claiming to be the only genuine Brazilians: the 'real patriots'.

The 'yellow' footballing outcomes

The consequences of this 'war of colours' was both longstanding and multifaceted. They continue to have an impact not only in the country's footballing scene, but also in its daily political life, threatening both the future of democracy in Brazil and on the whole South American continent. All this political havoc made regular citizens start to question their unconditional love for the national team. Examples of this detachment towards the Seleção are countless and can be seen in simple everyday gestures. In 2018 for instance just before the Russia World Cup, a small but symbolic incident revealed the apathetic mindset towards the Seleção in a poor and tiny neighbourhood in Teresina, the capital city of Piaui, a State in the Brazilian north. Instead of painting their streets and houses with Brazil's national colours (yellow and green) and instead of decorating their houses with the Brazilian flag, the Teresina residents coated and ornamented everything with the colours of Argentina, Brazil's fiercest sporting rivals!

People who have lived long enough to witness the traditional *carnivalesque* atmosphere that used to take over the country's streets during Brazilian matches in any World Cup during the 20th century and the early 2000s say that this party mood has been slowly subsiding in the last two World Cups (Russia and Qatar). In the past, as the Seleção played an international match in the Copa America or the World Cup, the country would basically stop. Schools, universities, shops, bank branches, and even courts would close for the day. The only question to ask was: where are you watching 'the match'? People used to have barbecues and organise small or large parties at their houses to gather friends and neighbours to watch. In the worst-case scenario, when you could not just shut a business or a school door, the management of these organizations would assemble a large screen in a hall so everyone could watch and to ensure that their 'national duty' of cheering for the Seleção was accomplished.

Nowadays, more and more people do not show this level of interest in the team anymore. Reports are that people just go to work, and offices, schools, and bank branches remain open during the Seleção's matches. It looks like the 'war of colours' took its toll and that, combined with the most recent FIFA scandals (where three former presidents of the Brazilian Football Federation (CBF) were expelled from their positions, banned from football by FIFA and even incarcerated in the US), it has resulted in one major legacy: the importance of the Seleção started to be questioned and since then the team has ceased to be at the centre of many people's everyday lives.

Recent polls show that 41% of Brazilians do not care about football anymore. Moreover, there is an increasing tendency from some to barrack *against* the national team.

The yellow threat to civilization as we know it

Since Dilma Rousseff's impeachment campaign, the use of the Seleção's yellow jersey for partisan reasons has continued in the political life of Brazil. In 2018, just after the Russia World Cup, a fierce national election campaign took place in the country. In October of the same year, Brazilians went to the polls to vote for their President, part of the Senate (high-chamber), the entire low-chamber (513 representatives), State Governors and State representatives. These major elections happen every four years in the country, matching with the World Cup calendar, and usually people and the media pay much more attention to the Presidential elections than to the elections to the other roles.

That year was no different. With former President Lula, the leader in all electoral polls, incarcerated by Operation Car Wash, Jair Bolsonaro, an obscure far-right Federal representative from Rio de Janeiro, emerged as one of the main contenders for the Presidential chair. Lula's Workers' Party and other political parties from a range of ideological spectrums also presented their candidates. However, Bolsonaro's campaign was totally different from anything the country had seen since democratic life returned to Brazil in the late 1980s. His electoral crusade was marked by an intense use of fake news across several social media channels, and his aggressive speeches spread hate against all social minorities—in every single media appearance, interview or occasional conversation, Bolsonaro's rants targeted black and Indigenous communities, gender-diverse people, women, and lower classes.

Moreover, Bolsonaro's campaign was marked by a distinctive uniform: the

Seleção's yellow jersey. His supporters were quick to claim 'ownership' of the national team's shirt. As Bolsonaro presented himself as the representative of the so-called 'new politics' and the true and only 'anti-corruption' candidate, it was a remarkable paradox seeing his supporters wearing a jersey identified with one of the most corrupt sporting bodies in the world; a football federation that had its former presidents either jailed in the US during that period of time or in fear of leaving the country and being caught by the FBI due to their outstanding corruption accusations. Such an irony did not bother Bolsonaro's supporters: they sported the yellow jersey to prove their patriotism and as part of their mission to quash the Workers' Party—and all its social policies and allegedly corrupt practices—from the political life of the country.

As Bolsonaro stepped into the Presidential office in 2019, the yellow jersey became the major symbol of his government. His term (until 2022) was marked by constant political tension; he promoted several political rallies across the country where a sea of yellow jerseys could be seen on the streets. Some verbal altercations and physical clashes started to happen across Brazilian cities, usually featuring Bolsonaro's supporters (*bolsonaristas*) who faced opponents of his policies and bigoted ideologies. A few of these adversaries wore red jerseys, but the President's cliques were easily recognizable wearing the Seleção's yellow jersey. These clashes led to another noticeable movement: many Brazilians stopped wearing their beloved team's jersey out of fear of being identified as a Bolsonaro follower, which could endanger their safety.

Realizing these changes and how Brazilian fans were not wearing the famous '*amarelinha*' (the Seleção's 'number one' yellow jersey), Nike, the jersey's sponsor and maker, started to produce more of the team's 'number two' jersey—the blue ones. The yellow jersey quickly became a visible sign of '*bolsonarismo*', a political ideology that was more than a threat to democracy: it was questioning the electoral system, and every single Supreme Court decision, hence destroying the foundations of the Brazilian Republic. *Bolsonarismo* was also ripping apart any sort of social support to the lower classes, creating hunting clubs to facilitate access to guns, denying healthcare during the COVID-19 pandemic and putting the Amazon Rainforest's existence in real danger, along with the lives of its native populations.

As the 2022 Qatar World Cup approached, the national elections were on

Brazil's political agenda. A new social phenomenon began—yet again involving the yellow jersey. Frustrated with the 'kidnapping' of one of their major national symbols by the far right, some citizens customized their own yellow jersey with the name and number of their favourite politician or Presidential candidate. They began to lose their fear of wearing a yellow jersey on the streets or displaying it on their social media. Usually, these uniforms were stamped with "Lula-13" as he had already been released from jail and was again running for office.

However, many citizens were either still afraid or unwilling to wear the Seleção's number one uniform. Their fear was justified because as the general election day grew closer, Bolsonaro's supporters became more aggressive. Ignited by political arguments, fights started to happen in pubs and on the streets. Facilitated by Bolsonaro's pro-gun policies, shootings and even murderers were committed against 'red-wearing people'. Many of Bolsonaro's opponents did not want to wear red colours and symbols for fear of being attacked by crazy and violent *bolsonaristas;* nor did they want to wear the yellow shirt for fear of being seen as *bolsonaristas.*

In the usual FIFA calendar, the World Cup takes place before the October Brazilian general elections. However, as the Qatar World Cup was played in November and December, Bolsonaro had already lost the 2022 Presidential election by a tiny margin when the tournament began. As the Brazilian team's matches approached, a new and even more interesting phenomenon started to happen to symbolize the relationship between Brazilian fans and their jersey: the customization of the Seleção's jersey using different formats and colours. As football supporters felt that new and better winds were blowing in the country after Bolsonaro's downfall, they started to tailor the jersey with different colours; red, purple and even LGBTQ+ rainbow Seleção jerseys appeared on the market, further showing the deep connection between football and the country's political and social life.

Is there a yellow future?

Despite losing the election, Bolsonaro never conceded defeat after the elections. Even though he received nearly 57 million votes, after his loss he remained in his office without a word to the media or his supporters. Some claim he was planning a coup d'état; others realized that he was truly depressed and afraid of his future as he knew he would be prosecuted and probably incarcerated for the numerous crimes he had committed both before and during his Presidential term.

However, his supporters did not stay quiet. Motivated by widespread fake news that the elections were somehow fraudulent, and that Bolsonaro was robbed by the powers that be, just after the voting in late October 2022 the *bolsonaristas* camped around the army headquarters across the country's main cities for months. They begged the military for an 'intervention' that would prevent Lula from taking the Presidential office—the official Presidential inauguration ceremony always happens on the first day of the year after the election. These *bolsonarista* camps were well-structured with chemical toilets, kitchens, and large, expensive tents. A distinctive feature of these camps was the ostensive presence of the national team's yellow jersey; the so-called 'patriots' insisted on wearing the national colours in their ongoing mission of saving the country from Lula, his political party, the corruption and the 'communism'.

More interesting and somehow comic was a phenomenon that occurred inside these camps—as Brazil started their football campaign in the Qatar World Cup, the *bolsonaristas* did not even want to watch the Seleção's performances in Qatar. Their focus was campaigning for a military coup to reinstitute 'order' in the country, so they banned any kind of World Cup broadcast inside their camps. Despite wearing the Seleção's yellow jerseys, they argued that they had more important things to worry about than watching mere football matches!

On the other hand, regular Seleção supporters started to display Brazilian flags in their houses and apartment windows and wear the Seleção's yellow jersey once more, but with a clear caveat: "I'm not a *bolsonarista*, this is just for the World Cup!". At the same time, the CBF started a media campaign with videos trying to convince people that the yellow jersey should be seen as a symbol of a united country.

Brazil's 2022 World Cup campaign did not go as expected, but the *bolsonaristas*' camps remained in front of the army headquarters. Participants received food and even some financial support from right-wing businessmen associated with Bolsonaro's government. Two days before the end of his Presidential term, on 30 December 2022, Bolsonaro fled the country heading towards the US, and thus avoiding being part of Lula's Presidential inauguration. Just a week after this ceremony, on 8 January, the *bolsonaristas* camped in Brasilia (the Federal capital), marched on the city streets and invaded the Parliamentary houses, the Supreme Court building and the Presidential Palace. They broke windows and furniture, destroyed rare art works, urinated and defecated in the offices, and ruined the public and political heritage of these buildings, creating chaotic scenes in the capital city. As they had become the sign of the *bolsonaristas*' demonstrations, a sea of yellow jerseys was clearly seen as the vandals paraded in and out of these official buildings, posting their crimes in real time on their social media channels

After this mayhem, as police forces restored order in the Federal capital and the delinquents started to be jailed, the CBF's president met with Nike to discuss and plan the future of the national team's jersey. Many Brazilian fans thought they would change the number one jersey to a white one which had been the traditional jersey that the team wore until the 1950 *Maracanazo*. This could be a smart move, as the country's latest political scenario has shown that the yellow jersey is now a far-right political symbol. After all, as FIFA does not want and often prohibits political messages from being displayed on players' uniforms, why doesn't it ban the Brazilian yellow jersey?

Once a symbol of the *jogo bonito* and a sign of Brazilian-ness, the yellow jersey has become part of another massive narrative since the 2014 World Cup. Instead of promoting unity and celebration through football to Brazilians, it has brought division and distress. Perhaps the once beloved *'amarelinha'* has also become a symbol of Brazil's socially divided communities, where so few have so much, and most live on so little.

PART 3:
GLORY

CHAPTER 13

Glorious marvels of South America

Gorgeous! What a marvellous dance, this game of futebol!
—Mário de Andrade

South American football never fails to convey astounding stories to the football planet. These can be tales of passion, revolution, or glory. They show the ongoing potency of the game on the continent to the world —and its influence over the globe.

At the end of December 2022 while I was finishing the first draft of this book, South American football again brought shockwaves all over the world. The first of these 'football tsunamis' was made up of days of pure bliss, causing a state of ecstasy that spread from Argentina to the Middle East and back—Argentina's and Messi's World Cup title.

The second 'December tidal wave', although originating in the core of South America, also spread around the entire planet. It gained headlines in media outlets on every single continent. Unlike the first one though, this second wave caused agony and sadness for billions of people—the passing of Pelé

I decided to close this book with a tribute to these two football geniuses from my continent.

One Scaloneta, two Lionels

Since 1986, Argentinians had been impatiently waiting for a moment, as described by Argentinian sociologist Pablo Alabarces, of pure *felisidá* (joyfulness) that reached and traversed all genders, social classes, and age groups in society. It had been 36 years since Maradona used his *Mano de Dios* (God's hand) to lift the World Cup trophy for the *Albiceleste* team. They had since appeared in two World Cup Finals, losing against West Germany in Italy (1990), and losing after extra time against Germany in Brazil (2014).

Lionel Messi, a consecrated player who did not need to prove anything else in football, wasn't a unanimous hero in his country until the Qatar campaign. Many of his countrymen whimpered about his lack of patriotism, as if he was not that interested in the national team, and never gave everything he had for the Albiceleste shirt. Even though he led the 2014 team to the World Cup Final, his grandfather appeared on TV after that defeat saying he was a "bit lazy"

Messi qualifies this 2014 defeat against the Germans the saddest moment he ever lived on a football pitch. In a 2023 recorded conversation with Zinedine Zidane, Messi declared, that although the 2022 win in Qatar has eased a bit that pain, the 2014 *espinita* (little thorn) will always be there. One of the most famous images of that tournament is the picture of a shocked Lionel Messi watching from a close range the World Cup trophy, without being able to touch it. There was a five-year gap before Messi played again in the Maracanã stadium, during the 2019 Copa America quarterfinals against Venezuela. However, the image that marked Messi's involvement in the competition took place in the third-spot decision: after a dispute with Chilean Gary Medel, both ended up excluded. It was the first red card of Messi's career since 2005.

Between the 2014 painful defeat and this red card in 2019, Messi's time with the Argentinian team was instable. They lost two continental finals against Chile: in the 2015 Copa America and in the 2016 Copa America *Centenario* (hundred-year anniversary). After those defeats and under fire for 'not giving everything to the National Team's jersey', a tired Messi declared that his time with the Argentinian team 'was over'.

However, after three months he was back to help the team to conquer a place in the 2018 World Cup finals. After a shameful campaign at the Russia World Cup (2018) when they were eliminated in the round of 16, Messi again considered retiring from the national team. He stayed away of the last three friendly matches the team played on that year.

On those days, the Argentinian Federation (AFA) wanted to renew the team and provide opportunities for younger players with good prospects to build their careers and fame abroad. When not many coaches put their hands up for the challenges of saying farewell to the big stars of the team, the AFA called Lionel Scaloni, a young man with an impressive curriculum as a player, but who was just at the beginning of his coaching career. There was no fanfare when *La Scaloneta* (Scaloni's little team) was born. On the contrary, Scaloni and his young group of players were heavily criticized by both the Argentinian mainstream media and a large portion of their fans. When discussing football, South Americans can be overly critical, harsh, and sometimes cruel. Argentinians are masters of moans against their national team, coach, and players.

Everyone involved with *La Scaloneta* wanted to prove their critics wrong. Step by step, and before becoming a symbol of hope, *La Scaloneta* was already a sign of resistance. Taking a further step, Scaloni persuaded Messi to return to the team. That was the right decision. After the red card at the 2019 Copa America, he came back to Brazil to help the Argentinians to win the 2021 Copa America, beating the home team in the Final. Due to Covid-19 restrictions, that match was played in front of an empty Maracanã stadium. Still on the pitch, Messi made a videocall to his parents, wife, and children to celebrate this special moment with his family.

Close friends of Messi have no doubt in stating that the Qatar world title started to emerge that night, on the grass of a quiet Maracanã, minutes after that videocall. During that tournament, Messi had grown as a leader for the young *Scaloneta* boys. Slowly, an initially invisible alliance between Argentinian *hinchas* (supporters), the media, Messi and *La Scaloneta* started to grow.

This positive vibe could represent the 'missing link' for the Argentine team. After all, fans around the world wanted Lionel Messi to crown his career with a World Cup title. But many in Argentina still doubted his real loyalty to their nation. As an optimistic atmosphere grew within the country, *hinchas* started to display more enthusiasm and trust in the team. A few months before the tournament, the hinchas put a new chant together to support the team that quickly went viral on the internet. With a contagious beat, it sings, "Lionel (Messi), you deserve this Cup, let's go *La Scaloneta* win the matches, we don't want anything without Lio (Messi)." [3]

---

[3] To listen to the original, search for 'Lionel esta copa te la mereces'.

Fabricio Rodriguez is a middle-aged football fan who migrated to Australia from Argentina during his adolescence. In his social media profile, he describes himself as an "Argentinian-Australian". During the group stage of the Qatar World Cup, just before the match between Fabricio's two countries, he posted his picture on social media wearing an Albiceleste jersey and a Socceroos' headscarf. His caption read: "Argentinian is who I am; Australian is who I've become; don't ask me to explain it." I completely understand Fabricio, as I see that every migrant has two hearts.

Nevertheless, as the tournament progressed, Fabricio incorporated the *La Scaloneta* spirit, and on his social media posts he started to translate aspects of his football culture, always stating that "We Argentinians do…". Just a few days after Argentina's win over France in the penalty shootout, we exchanged a few text messages. They were great South American brotherhood talks. In one of these messages, my *hermano* (brother) Fabricio told me: "I might be over playing it here. But I will say it anyway. I can't think of many other events in human history, be it sporting or otherwise, where so much collective good was channeled towards one person to win something like people felt in this World Cup and Messi! Unbelievable!".

Fabricio's words capture the spirit that embraced this Argentinian team during the Qatar World Cup. After a shocking defeat against underdogs Saudi Arabia in their opening match, their coach was not afraid to change his tactics and choose a different line-up for each game, adjusting his team to the opponent's tactics. Lionel Scaloni proved to be an independent thinker who can not only read, but also write the game.

While the team's nickname gave well-deserved recognition to Lionel Scaloni's fine efforts with the group, *La Scaloneta* would never have worked as well as it did without the genius of the 'other' Lionel. During each game Messi marvelled the world with his precise touches, his incredible assists, his goals, and his unbelievable dribbles that left the world's better defenders behind. Further, for those who enjoy keeping an eye on the tactics of the game, it was a delight to see how Messi managed to adjust his positioning to what his team needed: he played as 'false 9', but also occupied different spots on the field, making the task of marking him absolutely problematic. Messi controlled the tempo of matches even when he did not have the ball; he would often stop and just wait away from the defenders, in spaces only he can see on the field. There, he either attracted defenders' attention, leaving more room for his teammates, or he made himself available to receive the ball and give it a sudden acceleration.

The World Cup Gods would never sleep well if Messi hadn't achieved the glory of lifting the trophy.

In addition to his football feats, Lionel Messi has always been deeply supportive of relevant social causes in his country, such as the *Abuelas de Plaza de Mayo* (Grandmothers of Plaza de Mayo). This social movement has its origins within the *Madres de Plaza de Mayo* movement. The *Madres* (mothers) have gathered daily in front of the Presidential Palace in Buenos Aires to protest against the violences inflicted to their children by the dictatorship since the mid-1970s. The *Abuelas* was founded in the mid-1980s with the specific aim to investigate the fate of babies who were born in jail and subsequently stolen from their mothers, adopted and raised by families associated to the military. The *Abuelas* group conducts rigorous investigations to uncover the identity of grandchildren who were raised by these families. Just before embarking to the Brazil World Cup, Messi lead a group of national players to support a new media campaign of the Abuelas. In their 2014 campaign, Messi appeared in photos and videos with the Abuelas leadership, holding a placard saying *Resolvé tu identidad ahora* (Resolve your identity now), which aims to encourage people to be upfront if they have questions about their family roots. At the end of the video Messi says the campaign slogan: *Hace 10 mundiales que te estamos buscando* (We have been looking for you for 10 World Cups). The Abuelas de Plaza de Mayo had already recovered the identify of more than 100 children who were kidnapped by the dictatorship. They are still looking for other 200 kidnapped babies.

Edson King Pelé do Nascimento

A few days after the end of the Qatar World Cup, on 29 December 2022, while South America was still celebrating the return of the World Cup trophy to the continent where the global tournament was first played, we were all suddenly compelled to end the commemorations. The immense joy of Argentina's win was quickly replaced by deep sadness as the news of the death of the King of

Football quickly travelled around the world.

Pelé's passing became instantly the world's 'hot topic'. Nobody seemed to be able to talk about anything else. On the internet, social media, TV shows, and large and small media outlets—everywhere you looked—he was the main news.

The major newspapers in almost every part of the planet stamped his death on their covers. *"Il était un roi"*—"He was a King"—read the headline in the French *L'équipe*; among other grandiose terms, the word "King" was a constant alongside large pictures of Pelé that covered nearly the entire front pages of media outlets in every continent. Even the *Diário Clarín*, the largest Argentine newspaper, was bound to drop the everlasting comparisons between Pelé, Messi, and Maradona, to concede that "the supreme symbol of football has died".

In Brazil, O Globo, one of the three most relevant national daily newspapers, printed an unprecedented issue to celebrate Pelé's life. This special edition had four different covers, each picturing an iconic moment of the King's brilliant career: a young Pelé juggling the ball with his head in a training session during the 1958 Sweden World Cup; the King dribbling an opponent in the 1962 Chile World Cup before the injury that forced him to leave the competition; Pelé in the arms of Jairzinho, smiling and celebrating a goal in the 1970 Mexico World Cup; and the crowd carrying Pelé on their shoulders after he scored his 1,000th goal in the Maracanã Stadium in 1969. Each cover had the same headline, either above or below the King's picture: *"Pelé eternal"*.

The even-numbered years on the covers of *O Globo* represented the three World Cups he won; the only player to have achieved such a feat. The celebration of his 1,000th goal, though, in 1969, brings us to an interesting story about the man who was elected in 1980 the '20th century athlete'. As Pelé's life has already been dissected from every single angle, and almost everything that could be said about him has already been said, perhaps a discussion of this record goal shows another facet of the King that is worth exploring.

The 1,000th goal and the politics of Pelé

On 15 October 1969, Santos beat Portuguesa de Desportos 6–2 in a match for the Brazilian Championship, then called *Torneio Roberto Gomes Pedrosa*. On that afternoon in the Pacaembu Stadium, Pelé scored four goals against the team from the Portuguese community. From that day, the countdown began. Pelé had reached 993 career goals, and the following matches generated immense attention both across the country and around the world. Everyone wanted to see the King round up his goal tally. When it rose to 996, Santos travelled to the northeast of the country for a three-game streak against not-so-strong sides. As the likelihood of him scoring his 1,000th goal was so enormous, the host cities were already preparing their parties for the big occasion. After the first match, Pelé's tally reached 998—just two more!

The team then arrived in João Pessoa, the capital city of Paraiba. There was a large party waiting for them at the airport. The city's Mayor presented Pelé with the title of Honorary Citizen of João Pessoa. Shortly after the match started, Santos was already beating Botafogo-PB 2-0 when they received a penalty, and a euphoric crowd began to scream Pelé's name. Even though he was not the official penalty shooter of the team, he felt compelled to take the shot: 999 goals!

It looked like his 1,000th goal would be scored in that match—away from the media of Rio de Janeiro or São Paulo. However, as everybody in Santos FC wanted the milestone to be achieved and celebrated in the Maracanã Stadium, Julio Mazzei—then Santos' coach and the man who later would bring Pelé to the North American Soccer League to play for the NY Cosmos—put his alternate plan into action: goalkeeper Jair Estevão fell, groaning in pain. There was no reserve keeper on the team's bench, and the official substitute goalkeeper, both for Santos and the Seleção, was Pelé, who was moved to the keeper position and did not score another goal that day.

Yet before playing Vasco in the Maracanã Stadium, Santos had to face EC Bahia in Salvador in their packed stadium. Nobody told Pelé that he should save his landmark goal for the following match—the King was anxious to score to be free from the pressure. He really tried to notch a goal in that match—he had two amazing opportunities, and the last one was saved by a defender on the goal line after the keeper was already beaten. Interestingly, the local crowd, instead of celebrating, booed Nildo—the defender who prevented the goal.

Then, the night of 19 November arrived. 70,000 paying people, plus nearly 30,000 among 'authorities'—the ones who could just make their way into the crowd without a paying ticket—packed the Maracanã to witness Santos playing Vasco da Gama, one of the four major clubs in Rio de Janeiro. Vasco players spent the whole week of their match preparations joking with Andrada, the Argentine goalkeeper of their team. Andrada had an ankle injury, and they mocked that he was afraid to be on the receiving end of the famous goal. But after a medical examination in the locker room, Andrada decided to play—and he did it so well!

Vasco players did not 'cooperate' with the party. Beneti opened the scoring in the first half for the local team. Andrada was having a brilliant night and made a miraculous leap to block a mid-range position shot from Pelé. The score was even when at the 32nd minute of the second half, the referee 'found' a penalty for Santos. Despite the complaints of the Vasco players, and with no VAR to validate the fault (or not), the penalty was confirmed. The stadium was silent. Santos players gathered in the mid-field; curiously, Vasco's football director was holding a Vasco jersey in his hands with the number 1,000 on the back—the same jersey that Pelé wore as he did his lap around the stadium after the goal.

Andrada jumped to the right side and almost spoiled the party, but the ball found the back of the net, and the rest is history. The game was interrupted, a crowd of journalists invaded the field, and Pelé was carried on the shoulders of his teammates. Still inside the field, in front of dozens of microphones, a visibly touched Pelé made a statement that would haunt him for the rest of his life:

> "In this moment of great emotion for me, I say that I owe everything that I am to the Brazilian people. And I appeal to you never to forget poor children, the needy and charities. Let's stand up for the poor, let's stand up for little children in need".

We need to remember that in 1969 Brazil was under a ferocious dictatorship. While the army took power in 1964, it wasn't until 1968 that the regime really escalated. In December 1968, then President and army General Costa e Silva decreed the AI-5, a bill that closed Parliament, reinforced censorship and torture as regular practices of the authoritarian government, and revoked the political rights of hundreds of citizens.

It was within this context that Pelé made his statement in front of the world's cameras. After that, over many years and decades, several social movements criticized him for not making a speech against racism. After all, as a black person with such visibility, the anti-racism militants firmly believed that Pelé should have been much more active on this issue. But, according to them, Pelé never really stepped up to fight for more than just poor children.

Pelé was always questioned for not having a more active political stance, either against the dictatorship or against racism. As if his football achievements weren't enough, as if being such a talented, world-famous black athlete did not give plenty of inspiration to African-descendent children around the globe, many Brazilians always found something to criticize him about.

However, there were several instances when Pelé did make relevant political points. For example, in 1984 as the whole country was protesting on the streets to demand Presidential elections (the "Free Elections Now!" campaign), he graced the cover of *Placar*, then the most relevant Brazilian sports magazine. In an iconic and unusual picture, Pelé was wearing a classic hat and sporting a moustache, and he also wore a yellow shirt with the symbol of the CBD (the Brazilian Football Confederation), and large black words on the front of his shirt: 'FREE ELECTIONS NOW!' An important detail here is that yellow was not only the colour of the Seleção's jersey but also the colour of the 'Free Elections Now!' movement, so this combination on Pelé's picture was a great match.

In a 1995 interview on the highly acclaimed and popular *Jô Soares* talk show, Pelé told two stories that reveal how he lived with the pressure of further political engagement. At that time, he was Minister of Sport and helped to pass a Parliamentary bill that ended the *lei do passe* (the license law) that made professional football players almost slaves of their clubs, even after their contracts expired. The bill, later known as the 'Pelé Law', also brought a range of benefits for athletes who played other Olympic sports.

In that interview, he said that as a Minister, he had a meeting in Brasilia with a range of leaders of the anti-racism and black social movements. When asked what he would do to fight racism, he responded that he would personally work to elect more black State and Federal representatives, as he thought only black people would care for their own interests.

Pelé also revealed an interesting fact about his 1,000[th] goal. It was 11:30 pm when he scored that remarkable goal—in another half hour it would have been his mother's birthday. He told Jô Soares that it would have been much easier for him to just dedicate that goal to his mum alone, so as not to create controversies with anyone. Nevertheless, he said what he said to all those microphones as he felt an enormous commitment to underprivileged Brazilian children, and claimed he would never regret that statement, even though it generated plenty of criticism towards him during his life.

Pelé used to refer to himself in the third person. He used to say, "Pelé did that, and Edson thought that." (Pelé was a nickname, his full name was Edson Arantes do Nascimento). He knew that as a footballer he was a king, an idol around the world, and considered everywhere as the perfect athlete. But Edson was a citizen like any other who had failures and made mistakes that were magnified by his status. We must also remember that both Pelé and Edson were victims of racism, and many times in his early career he was described in the media as a "black person with a white soul".

> *"Michael Jordan is the Pelé of basketball. Muhammad Ali is the Pelé of boxing. Beethoven is the Pelé of classic music. Marta is 'the Pelé in skirts' (kinda sexist, but you get my point here). Pelé is the Pelé of football. Messi GOAT but is yet to become an adjective of royalty."*

This was my tweet when I heard the gloomy news of Pelé's passing. I did not want to create new controversies with my Argentinian *hermanos* (brothers) with this post. Contrary to the general belief, many Brazilians, including myself, clearly supported the *Albiceleste* in the Qatar World Cup Final, and we were very happy for their victory. There is already plenty of healthy—and some unhealthy—banter between Brazilian and Argentinian football supporters. One of the funniest chants that Argentinians brought to the 2014 Brazil World Cup ended with the line, "Maradona is better than Pelé", to which Brazilian fans responded by creating another chant that said, "Pelé has more Cups than you" (that now clearly needs some updates).

***

Pelé and Messi are football geniuses, who not only made South Americans happy and proud, but also elevated the profile of our continent in the world. They astonished the world with their unparalleled skills.

They are two South American wonders who will forever bring glory to our continent.

References

Aguilar-Aguilar, E. and Alcazár-Campos, A. (2022) 'Bolivian Women as Professional Footballers: The Voices and the Feminism of the karimachus' in J. Knijnik and G. Garton (eds) *Women's Football in Latin America: Social Challenges and Historical Perspectives Vol 2 Hispanic Countries*. Cham, Switzerland: Palgrave Macmillan, pp. 115–130.

Alabarces, P. (2008) *Fútbol y patria: El Fútbol y las narrativas de la nación en la Argentina*. Buenos Aires: Prometeo Libros.

Alabarces, P. (2014) *Héroes, machos y patriotas: El fútbol entre la violencia y los medios*. Buenos Aires: Aguilar.

Andrade, M. (1963) "Brasil-Argentina," in *Os filhos da Candinha*. São Paulo, SP: Martins Editora.

Archetti, E.P. (1992) "Argentinian football: A ritual of violence?" *The International Journal of the History of Sport*, 9(2), pp. 209–235.

Bellos, A. (2002) *Futebol: The Brazilian Way of Life*. London: Bloomsbury.

Benzecry, C.E. (2008) "Azul y Oro: The many social lives of a football jersey," *Theory, Culture & Society*, 25(1), pp. 49–76.

Bertoncelo, E.R. (2009) "'Eu quero votar para presidente': Uma Análise sobre a campanha das diretas," *Lua Nova: Revista de Cultura e Política*, (76), pp. 169–196.

Borges, J.L. (1984) "Blindness," in *Seven Nights*. New York, NY: New Directions.

Di Salvo, A.L. (2019) *Riquelme, El Torero*. Instituto de la caja.

Falcão, P.R. (2012) *Brasil 82 - O time que perdeu a copa e conquistou o mundo*. São Paulo, Editora Age.

Florenzano, J.P. (2010) *A Democracia Corinthiana: Práticas de liberdade no futebol brasileiro*. São Paulo: Educ/FAPESP.

Franco, J. (1992) "'Si me Permiten Hablar': La Lucha por el poder interpretativo," *Revista de Crítica Literaria Latinoamericana*, 18(36), pp. 111–118.

Frydenberg, J. (2013) *Historia social del fútbol: Del Amateurismo a La Profesionalización*. Buenos Aires: Siglo XXI.

Frydenberg, J.D. (2003) "Boca Juniors en Europa: El Diario Crítica y el primer nacionalismo Deportivo Argentino," *História: Questões & Debates*, 39(2), pp. 91–120.

Hijós, M.N. (2012) "Club Atlético Boca Juniors: reflexiones sobre la transformación de una asociación civil deportiva en una marca internacional," *EFDeportes.com, Revista Digital*, 17(174).

Horfshield. S. (2020). *1982 Brazil: The Glorious Failure*. Pitch Publishing.

Gaffney, C.T. (2010) *Temples of the Earthbound Gods: Stadiums in the Cultural Landscapes of Rio de Janeiro and Buenos Aires*. Austin, Texas: University of Texas Press.

Guano, E. (2002) "Spectacles of modernity: Transnational Imagination and local hegemonies in neoliberal Buenos Aires," *Cultural Anthropology*, 17(2), pp. 181–209.

Kittleson, R. (2014). *The Country of Football: Soccer and the Making of Modern Brazil*. University of California Press.

Knijnik, J. (2018) "Imagining a multicultural community in an everyday football carnival: Chants, identity and social resistance on Western Sydney terraces," *International Review for the Sociology of Sport*, 53(4), pp. 471–489.

Knijnik, J. (2018) *The World Cup Chronicles: 31 Days that Rocked Brazil*.: Balgowlah Heights, NSW, Australia, Fair Play Publishing.

Levinsky, S.A. (1996) *Maradona: Rebelde Con Causa*. Buenos Aires: Corregidor.

Macri, M., Ballvé, A. and Ibarra, A. (2009) *Pasión y Gestión: Claves del Ciclo Macri en Boca*. Buenos Aires: Aguilar.

Moreira, M.V.E. and Hijós, M.N. (2013) "Clubes deportivos, fútbol y mercantilización: los casos de Boca Juniors e Independiente en la Argentina," *Questión*, 1(37), pp. 149–162.

Nascimento, E.A. (2010) *Pelé - Minha Vida Em Imagens*. São Paulo: Cosac Naify.

Reis, D.A. (2010) "Ditadura, Anistia e Reconciliação," *Estudos Históricos (Rio de Janeiro)*, 23(45), pp. 171–186.

Segura M. Trejo, F. (2012) "Diego Armando Maradona: los Mundiales y la Política," *Istor*, (72), pp. 227–236.

Segura M. Trejo, F. (2013) "Diego Armando Maradona: vers une interprétation de la trajectoire de vie de l'icône," in J.F. Diana (ed.) *Spectacles sportifs, dispositifs d'écritures: Colloque*. Nancy: Press Universitaires de Lorraine, pp. 123–135.

Shirts, M. (1989) "Playing Soccer in Brazil: Sócrates, Corinthians, and Democracy," *The Wilson Quarterly (1976-)*, 13(2), pp. 119–123.

Sócrates (2012) *Sócrates, Brasileiro: As Crônicas do Doutor em Carta Capital*. Edited by S. Lirio. São Paulo, Brazil: Editora Confiança.

Sócrates and Gozzi, R. (2002) *Democracia Corintiana: A Utopia em Jogo*. São Paulo, SP: Boitempo.

Tavares, G.F.F. (2021) "O Dissidente Consciente," *Esporte e Sociedade*, (33).

Tomasi, D. (2014) *El Caño Más Bello del Mundo*. Buenos Aires: Hojas del Sur.

Vasconcellos, J. (ed.) (2010) *Recados da Bola: Depoimentos de Doze Mestres do Futebol Brasileiro*. São Paulo, SP: Cosac Naify.

Viezzer, M. (2013) *"Si me Permiten Hablar..." Testimonio de Domitila, una Mujer de las Minas de Bolivia*. Mexico: Siglo XXI Editores.

Wilde, N. (2009) "Interview with Orlando Salvestrini President of Marketing, Club Atletico Boca Juniors in Argentina," *International Journal of Sports Marketing and Sponsorship*, 10(3), pp. 2–6.

Wisnik, J.M. (2006) "The Riddle of Brazilian Soccer: Reflections on the Emancipatory Dimensions of Culture," *Review: Literature and Arts of the Americas*, 39(2), pp. 198–209.

Wisnik, J.M. (2008) *Veneno Remédio: O Futebol e o Brasil*. São Paulo, SP: Companhia das Letras.

Acknowledgments

Even though I am the sole person responsible for writing this book, a few people made crucial contributions to both its appearance and your readership.

Initially, I owe a great deal of gratitude to Bonita Mersiades, the publisher at Fair Play Publishing, for her trust in my ability to write another book in English about South American football. Since the 2018 publication of *The World Cup Chronicles: 31 Days that Rocked Brazil*, we have been fortunate to witness the growth of this niche publishing house. It consistently brings a range of amazing books covering every single aspect of the world game to football fans. Bonita has managed the development of her business with an accurate sense of aesthetics and remarkable quality control, not only opening an editorial avenue for football writers in Australia, but also bringing outstanding books to the public that otherwise would never be written (or published). *Muchas gracias* Bonita and all the Fair Play crew for your efforts with my manuscript.

I am also in debt to my dear friends MaguiLeo, Cleiton, Casco (Im Memoriam), Fabricio, Neilton, Sandronis, Dado, Chxica and Piva, for our incessant conversation about South American football, culture and politics. Thank you all for keeping my passion for the game alive! Words of gratitude go to Andy Harper, who took a few hours from his busy schedule as football commentator to read an early draft of this manuscript and produce an outstanding foreword for this book.

Last but not least, I want to acknowledge the very important role that my family plays in my writing; this book would not have seen daylight without the support, love and care I receive from my wife Selma and my adored children Marina, Luiza, Juliana and Alex.

About the Author

Dr Jorge Knijnik was born in Porto Alegre, the capital city of Rio Grande do Sul, Brazil's southernmost State. Due to the proximity of his home State to the Uruguayan and Argentinian borders, Jorge's family used to frequently drive to these two countries. It was during these travels that Jorge learnt some Spanish and developed a strong passion for South American cultures, and in particular, the continent's songs and footballing stories.

Jorge played as a central defender for the Yuracán FC where he used to follow his dad's football motto: "the ball can come through, never the striker". Jorge was never presented with the Belfort Duarte award!

He holds a PhD in Social Psychology from the Universidade de São Paulo (Brazil). In 2009 he migrated to Australia with his young family of six. Dr. Knijnik currently works as an Associate Professor in the School of Education and as a researcher in the Centre for Educational Research and the Institute for Culture and Society at Western Sydney University (New South Wales, Australia).

Jorge's most recent books are: *Historias Australianas: Cultura, Educação e Esporte do outro lado do mundo* (Fontoura); *Women's Football in Latin America: Social Challenges and Historical Perspectives* (Palgrave Macmillan) and *The World Cup Chronicles: 31 Days that Rocked Brazil* (Fair Play Publishing).

Twitter @JorgeKni

MORE REALLY GOOD BOOKS

Noddy, The Untold Story
of Adrian Alston

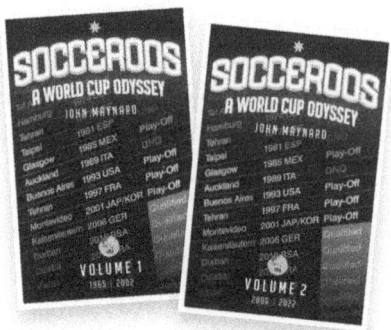

Socceroos – A World Cup Odyssey,
1965 to 2022 Volumes 1 and 2

Encyclopedia of Matildas
Beyond the World Cup 2023

George Best
Down Under

Woman Offside

Turning The Tide

Football Fans
In Their Own Write...

Hear Us Roar
– An anthology of
emerging women
football writers

Available from

fairplaypublishing.com.au/shop

and all

good bookstores

FAIRPLAY
PUBLISHING

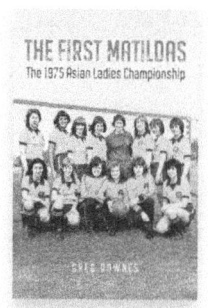

The First Matildas
The 1975 Asian
Ladies Championship

www.ingramcontent.com/pod-product-compliance
Lightning Source LLC
Chambersburg PA
CBHW041308110526
44590CB00028B/4290